Mystery of the MAZZAROTH
Prophecy in the Constellations

Tim Warner

MYSTERY of the MAZZAROTH

Second Edition
Copyright © 2013 by Tim Warner

All Scripture quotations, unless otherwise indicated, are from the New King James Version, Copyright © 1982 by Thomas Nelson, Inc. Used by permission. All rights reserved.

Contents

Introduction	1
1. Interpretations of the Zodiac	13
2. Ancient Sources	31
3. Virgo – The Abrahamic Covenant	41
4. Libra – The Law of Moses	61
5. Scorpio – The Sting of God's Rejection	71
6. Sagittarius – The Promised Land Realized	81
7. Capricorn – The Davidic Covenant	89
8. Aquarius – The Babylonian Exile	101
9. Pisces – The Return from Exile	107
10. Aries – The Lamb of the New Covenant	117
11. Taurus – The Apostolic Mission	127
12. Gemini – Gentiles Joined to Abraham's Seed	141
13. Cancer – The Tribulation	155
14. Leo – The King Reigns in Jerusalem	169
15. Epilogue	185
16. Preview of The TIME of the END	205

MYSTERY of the MAZZAROTH

Introduction

A study of the history and true meaning of the zodiac is probably one of the last things a Christian would want to do. The zodiac is used in the occult arts, astrology and fortune-telling. Such practices are forbidden in the Bible,[1] largely because they involve demonic spirits.[2]

Yet, the zodiac was not originally designed for such nefarious purposes. In His response to Job, God attributed the zodiac to Himself. *"Canst thou bind the sweet influences of Pleiades, or loose the bands of Orion? Canst thou bring forth __Mazzaroth__ in his season? Or canst thou guide Arcturus with his sons? Knowest thou the ordinances of heaven? Canst thou set the dominion thereof in the earth?"*[3] The answer was obvious. Job could not do these things—but God does.

The mysterious "Mazzaroth" mentioned in Job literally means "the twelve signs of the zodiac."[4] God claimed to bring out each of the twelve signs of the zodiac throughout the year in their proper months. It is hard to imagine God taking credit for something that originated in the minds of pagans. The Bible says that God is the one who named the stars. *"He counts the number of the stars; He calls them all by name. Great is our Lord, and mighty in power; His understanding is infinite."*[5]

---

[1] Leviticus 20:27
[2] Acts 16:16-19
[3] Job 38:31-33 KJV
[4] Brown Driver Briggs Hebrew Lexicon
[5] Psalm 147:4-5

MYSTERY of the MAZZAROTH

When God created the heavens, one of His stated purposes was to communicate to man through signs. Signs transcend language, culture, and generations. *"Let there be lights in the firmament of the heavens to divide the day from the night; and let them be for **signs** and seasons, and for days and years,"*[6] The Hebrew word translated "signs" is repeatedly used in Scripture to refer to symbols that represent a very specific message.

The same word is rendered "token" in reference to the rainbow, as a sign of God's covenant with Noah.[7] It was used of circumcision, the symbol of the covenant God made with Abraham.[8] The blood on the doorposts of the Israelites' houses on the first Passover was a "sign" that the inhabitants belonged to God.[9] The Sabbaths and festivals were "signs," each with a deep symbolic message.[10] Joshua used the same word when he commanded the Israelites to erect a monument of stones after God opened the Jordan River for them to cross, *"that this may be a **sign** among you when your children ask in time to come, saying, '**What do these stones mean to you?**' Then you shall answer them that the waters of the Jordan were cut off before the ark of the covenant of the LORD; when it crossed over the Jordan, the waters of the Jordan were cut off. And **these stones shall be for a memorial** to the children of Israel forever."*[11]

---

[6] Gen. 1:14
[7] Genesis 9:12, 13, 17
[8] Genesis 17:11
[9] Exodus 12:13
[10] Exodus 31:13-17
[11] Joshua 4:5-7

MYSTERY of the MAZZAROTH

As we see throughout Scripture and Biblical history, every "sign" has its corresponding meaning or message. That God created the constellations for signs means they each have a symbolic meaning; together they proclaim a very specific message which originated with God Himself.

King David was aware of a specific divine message broadcast to all mankind from the heavens.

> *Psalm 19:1-6*
> *1 The heavens declare the glory of God;*
> *And the firmament shows His handiwork.*
> *2 Day unto day utters speech,*
> *And night unto night reveals knowledge.*
> *3 There is no speech nor language*
> *Where their voice is not heard.*
> *4 Their line has gone out through all the earth,*
> *And their words to the end of the world.*
> *In them He has set a tabernacle for the sun,*
> *5 Which is like a bridegroom coming out of his chamber,*
> *And rejoices like a strong man to run its race.*
> *6 Its rising is from one end of heaven,*
> *And its circuit to the other end;*
> *And there is nothing hidden from its heat.*

God's awesome power, His infinite knowledge, and His stunning creativity can be seen in the diversity of life all around us and in the complexity and beauty of the systems within our world that support it. Yet, in this brief Psalm, David made no mention of living things, or the beauty of creation close at hand. These lyrics gushed forth from a heart pondering the magnificence of the heavens. To David, nothing compared to what he observed in the sky.

No doubt, as a boy tending sheep, David spent many nights in the fields gazing up at the starry hosts slowly marching across the expanse from east to west in perfect order. Yet, contrary to what we might expect from a shepherd-warrior-king, David's song does not merely reveal wonder and amazement at the grandeur and enormity of the heavens, or the military precision of its moving bodies. David's lyrics portray something that has eluded the average stargazer, even the Christian stargazer. David was in awe of a very specific message from the Creator that was continually broadcast across the heavens to all people of all languages. Night after night, month after month, year after year, the heavens are alive with a magnificent and intelligent proclamation: *"Day unto day utters speech, And night unto night reveals knowledge. There is no speech nor language Where their voice is not heard. Their line has gone out through all the earth, And their words to the end of the world."*

As with any language, there must be a common frame of reference between the speaker and the hearer. This is normally done with a common alphabet, vocabulary, and rules of grammar. All ancient writing began as pictures — pictographs. Egyptian hieroglyphics are a good example of pictograph writing. All letters of ancient alphabets began as simple drawings. The earliest form of written communication was a sequence of pictures, similar to "stick figures." To the ancients, a very simple picture had as precise a meaning as any word in our modern dictionaries. By arranging these simple drawings **in a specific sequence**, a message was communicated.

The twelve signs of the zodiac are a sequence of twelve pictures – a woman, a pair of scales, a scorpion, an archer, a goat-fish, a man holding a cauldron, two fish, a lamb, an ox, twin boys, a crab, and a lion. These twelve stick-figures march across the sky from east to west, taking a whole year to complete one cycle. Each month, the sun moves from one to the next, clothing it with light during the day, completely obscuring the stars of that sign for a month by illuminating our atmosphere.

The lyrics of Psalm 19 strongly imply that David understood the zodiac[12] – the circle of twelve constellations though which the sun passes each year. Those not familiar with basic astronomy might miss the clear connection between the constellations and the sun's dwelling in them. The "heavens" and the "firmament" are the fixed canvas on which the Creator has painted his masterpiece. The word "heavens" refers to the expanse of space through which the sun, moon, and planets run their courses. The "firmament" means something that is "fixed" or "firm," the visible things in the heavens that do not appear to move in relation to each other —the constellations. Yet David spoke specifically of the sun's path through the circuit of the twelve constellations of the

---

[12] The word "zodiac" comes from the Greek "ζωιδιακος," from "ζωη" (living) and "κυκλοω" (circle).

zodiac, known as the ecliptic.[13] He spoke of the sun's dwelling in a "chamber" or "tabernacle" within the constellations. *"In them* [the "heavens" and the "firmament"] *He has set **a tabernacle** for the sun, which is like a bridegroom coming out of his **chamber**, and rejoices like a strong man to run its race. Its rising is from one end of heaven, and its **circuit** to the other end."*

Some might suppose that David was merely observing the rising and setting of the sun, with the sun being hidden (in a chamber) at night. Yet, the Hebrew word rendered "chamber" is the same word used previously in Job in reference to the zodiac. *"He made the Bear, Orion, and the Pleiades, And the **chambers** of the south."*[14] That the twelve constellations of the zodiac are considered "chambers," "tabernacles," or "houses" for the sun is well known from ancient times. The same language is used in modern astrology. Job called the zodiacal constellations "chambers of the south" because he lived in the northern latitudes above the tropic of cancer. The sun was never directly overhead in its apparent path through the constellations. The sun's arc across the sky was always tilted toward the south.

David used the language of contemporary astronomy when he spoke of the sun's dwelling in each of the twelve "chambers," "tabernacles," or "houses" of the zodiac in its yearly "circuit" through the heavens. The sequence in which the twelve figures marched across the night sky, and the sun's

---

[13] The 'ecliptic' is defined by Webster as: *"That great circle of the celestial sphere which is the apparent path of the sun among the stars, or that of the earth as seen from the sun: the plane of the earth's orbit extended to meet the celestial sphere."*
[14] Job 9:9

movement from one chamber to the next, were critical to understanding the message that David saw in the heavens.

The sun's path in servicing each of the twelve signs indicates the direction in which they must be read. If each night David laid on his back with his feet to the south and head to the north, the twelve figures would slowly move across the night sky from left to right, meaning they would be read right to left (as the Hebrew language). Also, since the sun services the twelve zodiac constellations (one per month) in the same order, there can be no doubt about the sequence.

The Apostle Paul defined the message David said was proclaimed by the constellations. He quoted this very Psalm, naming the message which the heavens proclaim. This message contains the Gospel of Jesus Christ.

David:

> *Psalm 19:1-4 LXX[15]*
> *1 The heavens declare the glory of God; and the firmament proclaims the work of his hands.*
> *2 Day to day utters speech, and night to night proclaims knowledge.*
> *3 There are no speeches or words, in which their voices are not heard.*

---

[15] The "LXX" is the ancient Greek version of the Old Testament translated by 70 Jewish scholars about 300 years before the birth of Christ. It is called the "Septuagint," and was referred to by the early Christians as "the version of the seventy." Most quotations of the Old Testament by the Apostles in the New Testament were from this version, particularly by Paul. It is still used by the Greek-speaking churches.

> *4 Their sound has gone out to all the earth, and their words to the ends of the world.*

Paul:

> *Romans 10:16-18*
> *16 But they have not all obeyed <u>**the gospel**</u>. For Isaiah says, "LORD, who has believed our report?"*
> *17 So then faith comes by hearing, and hearing by the word of God.*
> *18 But I say, have they not heard? Yes indeed:*
> **"Their sound has gone out to all the earth, and their words to the ends of the world."**

David said a message was proclaimed by the sun's path through the constellations. Paul quoted David's Psalm as proof that the ancient nations had already heard the Gospel. Therefore the content of the message described by David included the Gospel of Jesus Christ.

In Romans 10, Paul applied David's Psalm about the message in the sky to the Gospel. In the first chapter he said God had actively made Himself known to mankind. Yet His message was corrupted by demons masquerading as gods,[16] and became the source of pagan mythologies, idolatry, and ultimately astrology. This corruption is the reason most Christians have shied away from contemplating the knowledge, power, and utterly amazing wisdom God has

---

[16] Deut. 32:17; 1 Cor. 10:20

demonstrated by foretelling His plan for mankind in the constellations.

> *Romans 1:18-25*
> *18 For the wrath of God is revealed from heaven against all ungodliness and unrighteousness of men, who suppress the truth in unrighteousness, 19 because what may be known of God is manifest in them, **for God has shown it to them**.*
> *20 For since the creation of the world His invisible attributes are clearly seen, **being understood by the things that are made, even His eternal power and Godhead**, so that they are without excuse, 21 because, although they knew God, they did not glorify Him as God, nor were thankful, but became futile in their thoughts, and their foolish hearts were darkened. 22 Professing to be wise, they became fools, 23 and changed the glory of the incorruptible God into an image made like corruptible man — and birds and four-footed animals and creeping things.*
> *24 Therefore God also gave them up to uncleanness, in the lusts of their hearts, to dishonor their bodies among themselves, 25 who exchanged the truth of God for the lie, and worshiped and served the creature rather than the Creator, who is blessed forever. Amen.*

It is a fact that many of the pagan idols were representations of the constellations. Paul did not view paganism as springing from multiple remote sources, but as the corruption and intentional degradation of a single divine revelation of God given to ancient man. God took the initiative to *show* the ancients the truth about Himself. The revelation of God was seen "since the creation of the world." Through willful ignorance, God's ancient revelation was perverted, driven by human lust. Divine knowledge was corrupted as men became *"futile in their thoughts, and their foolish hearts were darkened."* The true knowledge of God was "changed," becoming the source of pagan mythologies and carved images that represented them. The pagan myths, including those related to the zodiac, are corruptions of an original message given by God Himself to ancient man through the language of pictures.

Paul was an educated man, not only in the Jewish religion, but also in contemporary Greek thought. In his address to the philosophers at Athens, he seized on a thread of truth that still remained within the fabric of Greek pagan culture, citing from memory the Greek poet, Aratus, from his book on the constellations, *Phaenomena*.

> *Acts 17:26-29*
> *26 And He has made from one blood every nation of men to dwell on all the face of the earth, and has determined their preappointed times and the boundaries of their dwellings,*
> *27 so that they should seek the Lord, in the hope that they might grope for Him and find Him, though He is not far from each one of us; 28 for in Him we live and move and have our being, as also some of your own poets have said,* **'For we are also His offspring.'**
> *29 Therefore, since we are the offspring of God, we ought not to think that the Divine Nature is like gold or silver or stone, something shaped by art and man's devising.*

In the very paragraph Paul quoted, Aratus attributed the design of the zodiac to the supreme God (whom the Greeks called, "Zeus"). Below is the opening paragraph from Aratus' *Phenomena*. Paul's quotation is underlined.

> *"From Zeus let us begin; him do we mortals never leave unnamed; full of Zeus are all the streets and all the market-places of men; full is the sea and the havens thereof; always we all have need of Zeus.* <u>**For we are also his offspring**</u>*; and he in his kindness unto men giveth favourable signs and wakeneth the people to work, reminding them of livelihood. He tells what time the soil is best for the labour of the ox and for the mattock, and what time the seasons are favourable both for the planting of trees and for casting all manner of seeds.* **For himself it was who set the signs in heaven, and marked out the constellations**, *and for the year devised what stars chiefly should give to men right signs of the seasons, to the end that all things might grow unfailingly. Wherefore him do men ever worship first and last. Hail, O Father, mighty marvel, mighty blessing unto men. Hail to thee and to the Elder Race! Hail, ye Muses, right kindly, every one! But for me, too, in answer to my prayer direct all my lay, even as is meet, to tell the stars."*[17]

Paul did not seem to mind the implied connection between Zeus and the God of Israel. His discourse continues with a claim that an image he observed in Athens, dedicated to "the unknown God," represented the God he preached. Without question, Paul viewed the pagan religions of Athens as corruptions of the true ancient religion. Zeus was simply a corruption of the true God, the Creator of heaven and earth.

---

[17] Aratus, Phenomena, I

MYSTERY of the MAZZAROTH

Paul recognized that even within their corrupt paganism there remained smoking cinders of God's original message that had not been entirely snuffed out. Paul used these dying embers to kindle the flame of the Gospel of Jesus Christ in their midst.

Chapter 1
Interpretations of the Zodiac

Aratus, whom Paul quoted, attributed the zodiac to Zeus, the supreme god of the Greeks. The ancient Jewish historian, Josephus, writing around the time of Christ, wrote that ancient astronomy was a divine art, and was handed down by the sons of Seth.

> *"Now this Seth, when he was brought up, and came to those years in which he could discern what was good, became a virtuous man; and as he was himself of an excellent character, so did he leave children behind him who imitated his virtues. All these proved to be of good dispositions. They also inhabited the same country without dissensions, and in a happy condition, without any misfortunes falling upon them, till they died.* **They also were the inventors of that peculiar sort of wisdom which is concerned with the heavenly bodies, and their order.** *And that their inventions might not be lost before they were sufficiently known, upon Adam's prediction that the world was to be destroyed at one time by the force of fire, and at another time by the violence and quantity of water, they made two pillars, the one of brick, the other of stone: they inscribed their discoveries on them both, that in case the pillar of brick should be destroyed by the flood, the pillar of stone might remain, and exhibit those discoveries to mankind; and also*

inform them that there was another pillar of brick erected by them. Now this remains in the land of Siriad to this day."[18]

Since one tribe of righteous men cooperated in this particular discipline, and worked together to build monuments to preserve their knowledge of the heavens, they must have considered it to be vitally important. Josephus linked the Sethites' knowledge of astronomy with their knowledge of divine prophecy. They built monuments to preserve their celestial knowledge because of the prophecy of two future judgments, the flood and the judgment of fire. Peter linked these together as well in a passage that strongly hints at the very same tradition mentioned by Josephus.

> *2 Peter 3:5-7*
> *5 For this they willfully forget: that by the word of God the heavens were of old, and the earth standing out of water and in the water, 6 by which the world that then existed perished, being flooded with water. 7 But the heavens and the earth which are now preserved by the same word, are reserved for fire until the day of judgment and perdition of ungodly men.*

Some of the earliest Christians also believed the zodiac was divinely given. On the symbolism of the Ark of the Covenant, Clement of Alexandria wrote that the wings of the twin six-winged Cherubim adorning the ark of the covenant and the breastplate of the high priest symbolize the twelve signs of the zodiac.

---

[18] Josephus, *Antiquities*, Book I, ch. 2-3

> "And those golden figures, each of them with six wings, signify either the two bears, as some will have it, or rather the two hemispheres. And the name cherubim meant "much knowledge." But both together have twelve wings, and by the zodiac and time, which moves on it, point out the world of sense."
>
> "The twelve stones, set in four rows on the breast, describe for us the circle of the zodiac, in the four changes of the year." [19]

Hippolytus, disciple of Irenaeus, while strongly condemning the use of astrology to predict the future or discern one's fate, implied that the pagans have perverted the true and original meaning of the twelve signs of the zodiac.

> "But in each zodiacal sign they call limits of the stars those in which each of the stars, from any one quarter to another, can exert the greatest amount of influence; in regard of which there is among them, according to their writings, no mere casual divergency of opinion. ... Employing these (as analogies), Euphrates the Peratic, and Acembes the Carystian, and the rest of the crowd of these (speculators), **<u>imposing names different from the doctrine of the truth</u>**, speak of a sedition of Aeons, and of a revolt of good powers over to evil (ones), and of the concord of good with wicked (Aeons), calling them Taparchai and Proastioi, and very many other names. But the entire of this heresy, as attempted by them, I shall explain and refute when we come to treat of the subject of these (Aeons). But now, lest any one

---

[19] Clement of Alexandria, Stromata Bk. V, vi

> *suppose the opinions propounded by the Chaldeans respecting astrological doctrine to be trustworthy and secure, we shall not hesitate to furnish a brief refutation respecting these, establishing that the futile art [astrology] is calculated both to deceive and blind the soul indulging in vain expectations, rather than to profit it. And we urge our case with these, not according to any experience of the art, but from knowledge based on practical principles. Those who have cultivated the art, becoming disciples of the Chaldeans, and communicating mysteries as if strange and astonishing to men, **having changed the names** (merely), have from this source concocted their heresy."*[20]

Hippolytus indicated that the ancients' naming of the constellations, and connecting the stars in the forms of various figures, was never intended for the purpose of astrology (their influences over human fate), but rather as mnemonic devices.

> *"But I am rather of opinion, that the ancients imposed the names of received animals upon certain specified stars, for the purpose of knowing them better, not from any similarity of nature; for what have the seven stars, distant one from another, in common with a bear, or the five stars with the head of a dragon?"*[21]
>
> *"For, comparing the forms and dispositions of men with names of stars, how impotent their system is! For we know that those originally conversant with such investigations*

---

[20] Hippolytus, Refutation of All Heresies, Bk. IV, ii
[21] Hippolytus, Refutation of All Heresies, Bk. IV, vi

have called the stars by names given in reference to propriety of signification and facility for future recognition."[22]

An ancient Syrian Christian document asserts that the signs of the zodiac were created by God. It argues that man alone was given a free will, in contrast to all of the heavenly bodies.

*"But God in His benignity chose not so to make man; but by freedom He exalted him above many of His creatures, and even made him equal with the angels. For look at the sun, and the moon, **and the signs of the zodiac**, and all the other creatures which are greater than we in some points, and see how individual freedom has been denied them, and how **they are all fixed in their course by decree**, so that they may do that only which is decreed for them, and nothing else. ... But all these things are servants, and are subject to one decree: **for they are the instruments of the wisdom of God, which erreth not.**"*[23]

Ancient Jewish Interpretation of the Zodiac

Circular zodiacs have been found in several ancient Jewish synagogues in Israel, dating from the fifth century AD. They had mosaic tile floors portraying Bible stories in pictures. Yet, the most prominent place was reserved for a zodiac wheel with the twelve signs portrayed in picture as well as Aramaic or Greek script. The best-preserved examples are the Tzippori synagogue, the Hammat Tiberias synagogue, and the Beth Alpha synagogue.

---

[22] Hippolytus, Refutation of All Heresies, Bk. IV, xxvii
[23] Bardesan, Ante Nicene Fathers, Vol. VIII, p. 724

MYSTERY of the MAZZAROTH

Tzippori Synagogue[24]

---

[24] The Tzippori, and Hammat Tiberius zodiacs point to a date around 3,200 BC by the positions of the constellations in relation to the solstices and equinoxes (four women at the corners representing the four seasons). The summer solstice is aligned with Leo; the fall equinox is aligned with Scorpio; the winter solstice is aligned with Aquarius; and the Spring equinox is aligned with Taurus. All three synagogues have extensive Greek inscriptions. Greek-speaking Jews would naturally derive their chronologies and biblical dates from the Greek Septuagint translation of the Old Testament made about 250 BC. However, the ages of the patriarchs in the Septuagint (from the flood to Abraham) exceed the Hebrew dates by 880 years. Therefore, Jews using the Septuagint would date the flood 880 years too early, about 3200 BC. (The Beth Alpha zodiac was intended to depict the same date since two of the four are aligned the same as the other Jewish zodiacs. However, it was poorly and unevenly constructed, making it internally inconsistent). It is striking that all of these circular zodiacs, including the Egyptian Dendera zodiac, depict the four seasons as four women (Virgo – the only woman in the zodiac), and all four indicate the time of the flood when the four seasons first began (Gen. 8:22). The Dendera zodiac is based on Egyptian tradition that is independent of the Hebrew Torah, but agrees with it exactly regarding the date of

MYSTERY of the MAZZAROTH

Hammat Tiberias Synagogue[25]

The Jews either allegorized the signs or identified them with the twelve tribes of Israel.

> "Rabbinic authorities rationalized its (the Zodiac) inclusion (into prayer books) **by allegorizing the signs in terms of Jewish history** (Pesikta Rabbati 27-28)."[26]

> "According to the Yalkut Shimoni (Lev. 418), however, the standards of the 12 tribes correspond to the signs of the

---

the flood. The synagogue zodiacs are off by 880 years because of their dependence on the Septuagint.

[25] Photo by Bukvoed; http://en.wikipedia.org/wiki/File:Hamat-Tiberias-119.jpg

[26] Ellen Frankel & Betsy Platkin Teutsch, The Encyclopedia of Jewish Symbols, p. 199

zodiac. Thus in the east were stationed Juda, Issachar, and Zebulun, corresponding to Aries, Taurus, and Gemini; Reuben, Simon, and Gad in the south correspond to Cancer, Leo, and Virgo; Ephraim, Manasseh, and Benjamin in the west with Libra, Scorpio, and Sagittarius; and Dan, Asher, and Naphtali in the north with Capricorn, Aquarius, and Pisces."

"In the Pesikta Rabbati (27-28 ed. Freedman p. 133b) a passage occurs which explains the names of the signs homiletically in accordance with Jewish history. The Temple could not be destroyed in Nisan, since the ram which it represents in the zodiac is a reminder of the Akedah; Taurus is connected with the calf which Abraham slaughtered for his angelic guests (Ge. 18:7); the Gemini represent Jacob and Esau; while the Temple was destroyed in the month of Av, since its zodiacal sign Aryeh, the lion, corresponds to Ariel, the name given to the Temple (Isa. 29:1)."[27]

As the above quotation shows, the Jewish interpretation sometimes linked the twelve signs with Jewish history. But there was no specific order or meaning attached to the sun's sequential stay in each of the twelve houses of the zodiac, something critically important to the message David saw in the constellations. The Jewish interpretation relegated the zodiac to a kind of picture appendix to Israel's history in the Torah. Yet in this view, the constellations could tell no discernible story at all prior to, or independent of, the Torah. They were simply a grouping of random pictures. Just like the

---

[27] Encyclopedia Judaica, Keter Publishing House Jerusalem Ltd., 1972, Volume XVI, pages 1191-1192

pagan mythological interpretations of the zodiac signs, the complete lack of meaning to the sequence of the zodiac signs makes the Jewish interpretation doubtful and highly subjective.

Recent Christian Interpretations
Many have recognized similarities between the symbols in the Bible and the zodiac constellations, too many to be mere coincidence. The Scriptures which attribute the signs of the zodiac to God cannot be brushed aside. If God created them, named them, and used them as mnemonic devices to foretell His plan for the ages, their meaning ought to be discernible, particularly when we compare them to the symbols used in the Bible.

The first Christian attempt in fairly modern times to decipher the meaning of the zodiac symbols was made by Frances Rolleston, an expert in Semitic languages. She published her book, *"Mazzaroth, or the Constellations"* in London in 1862. Rolleston attempted to connect virtually all of the constellations with some aspect of the work of Jesus Christ in redemption. For example, Virgo was said to represent His Virgin birth. Libra (the scales) represented the price the Savior paid for sin. Scorpio (the scorpion) represented the sting of death which the Savior endured, etc. Rolleston justified these connections by tracing the phonetic sounds of some Arabic star names back to supposed Hebrew root words.

Yet, this process fails to consider that the Arabic names were fairly modern (from the Middle Ages), and largely reflect the position within the particular zodiac sign in the Arabic language. For example, "Denebola" in the constellation Leo simply means "tail of the Lion" in Arabic. "Ras Elased" in Leo simply means "forehead of the Lion" in Arabic. Instead of using the Arabic meanings (which were clearly meant to refer to that particular animal or sign), Rolleston attempted to redefine these words based on their similarity to Hebrew words in phonetic sound.

The entire process was very subjective, picking and choosing star names, and choosing similar sounding Hebrew words with which to link them. Such a process is extremely problematic since ancient Hebrew writing did not contain vowels, thus the exact pronunciation is not known for many ancient Hebrew words. This allowed Rolleston the flexibility to add any vowel sounds she chose in order to make these supposed connections. She assumed that the Arabic names selected were transliterations of ancient Hebrew words rather than originating in Arabic. Yet, the fact that the Arabic names make perfect sense in Arabic relating to the constellations in which they appear makes Rolleston's work in this regard highly suspect.

Rolleston's approach also made many constellations apply to Jesus Christ which did not exist in the most ancient star catalogues, but were added later by the Greeks or Romans. Interpreting these constellations as referring to Jesus Christ, using the same process (similarity in phonetic sound of Arabic star names to certain Hebrew words) makes the whole process appear subjective and forced. Since many of these constellations were identified rather late, how can they be connected to a single uniform prophecy given from the beginning?

Rolleston's book attracted little attention until it was discovered by Joseph Seiss, an American Lutheran minister in Philadelphia. Seiss was a Dispensationalist and heavily involved in Pyramidology. Many early Dispensationalists were fascinated with the Great Pyramid of Giza, thinking that its internal measurements pictured Dispensationalism's unique series of "dispensations." They believed the time of the alleged pretribulation rapture and the second coming of Christ could be discerned from the precise lengths of the various corridors and chambers within the Great Pyramid.[28] Seiss condensed Rolleston's work, publishing it as his own under the title, *"The Gospel in the Stars."* He contributed very little to Rolleston's original work, except presenting it in a more readable format.

Not to be outdone, E. W. Bullinger, another staunch Dispensationalist and contemporary of Seiss, published his own rehashing of Rolleston's work as *"The Witness of the Stars."* As with Seiss, Bullinger added nothing of significance or originality to what Rolleston had produced.

In more recent times, Rolleston's work has been repackaged by another Dispensationalist, Chuck Missler, again, with nothing of substance added to her work. Presbyterian minister, D. James Kennedy, also offered his own abridged knock-off of Rolleston's work. He was not a Dispensationalist,

---

[28] See Clarence Larkin's, "Dispensational Truth: God's Plan and Purpose in the Ages" for a good example of Dispensational Pyramidology.

but held to Reformed Theology which essentially holds that God is completely finished with Israel. Thus, like Dispensationalists, the zodiac signs were all forced to represent New Testament concepts exclusively.

The Jews interpreted the zodiac signs apart from any New Testament connection or reference to Jesus Christ. Dispensationalists, since they hold to a radical dichotomy between "Israel" and the "Church," interpreted the signs without regard for the Old Testament history of Israel. Both groups largely ignored the sequence of the signs, leaving them with random pictures.

More recently, apologetics and creation ministries have debunked the work of Frances Rolleston (and with it all of the other books based on her work), showing it as non-scientific and subjective, and rightly so.[29] These works have been convincing for many Christians who do not perceive the deficiencies underlying Rolleston's approach. Yet, like the "Bible Code" phenomenon, they fall short of persuading an honest skeptic.

The True Message in the Heavens
The basic premise of the former Christian works on the zodiac was undoubtedly correct—that God designed the zodiac to convey a message to humanity. The Bible states this plainly, but previous authors have apparently read into the constellations their own theological biases. These works either ignore Israel's role in God's redemptive plan (a Reformed

---

[29] http://www.answersingenesis.org/articles/am/v3/n1/gospel-in-stars

Theological bias), or isolate Israel from God's plan for His Church (a Dispensational bias).

All of these works completely ignore the most fundamental aspect of any prophetic message in symbols – that the sequence of the symbols tells a single story. A story requires a logical sequence to be read. Unless there is meaning to the order of the zodiac signs, David's observation cannot be correct. Without this order, the zodiac could not be read objectively by people of every language. It would simply be a grouping of random pictures open to any subjective interpretation.

The real story told by the zodiac deals with God's plan to restore His creation from His first divine act of restoration – the call of Abraham – until the consummation of Messiah's coming reign upon the earth. It is one story, not two. And it contains the message of both the Old and New Testaments in a unified whole. If the zodiac is prophecy, and if Israel's history is the conduit through which God has chosen to accomplish His ultimate goal, we would expect the zodiac to portray Jewish history sequentially from beginning to end.

One major failure of the Jewish interpretation was the omission of Jesus and His work of redemption found in the New Testament. Previous Christian interpretations have made the opposite mistake, omitting Israel's historical role in the Old Testament from God's plan of redemption. The message is more than just the death and resurrection of

MYSTERY of the MAZZAROTH

Christ. The Gospel of the Kingdom begins with the call of Abraham[30] and ends with the coming of Christ's Kingdom.

By comparing the zodiac signs to the history and prophecy of the Bible, it is evident that the zodiac tells the same story as the Bible in exactly the same sequence. It is the story of God's redemption of His creation using the nation of Israel as a conduit. It begins with the Abrahamic Covenant and takes us through all the major events in Jewish history recorded in the Old Testament. It then describes the story contained in the New Testament and concludes with Christ's future reign upon the earth. This story is told in the following sequence:

Old Testament
- Virgo: The Abrahamic Covenant (Gen.)
- Libra: The Mosaic Covenant (Ex. – Lev.)
- Scorpio: God's rejection of Israel (Num. – Deut.)
- Sagittarius: The Promised Land (Josh. – Jdgs.)
- Capricorn: The Davidic Covenant (Sam. – Chron.)
- Aquarius: The Babylonian exile (Isa. – Dan.)
- Pisces: The return from exile (Ezra – Neh., Hag. – Mal.)

New Testament
- Aries: The Lamb of the New Covenant (Matt. – Jn.)
- Taurus: The Apostolic mission (Acts)
- Gemini: Gentiles united with Israel (Rom. – Jude)
- Cancer: The great tribulation (Rev. 1-19)
- Leo: Messiah's Kingdom (Rev. 20-22)

---

[30] Gal. 3:8

Biblical prophecy uses the same pictorial language and symbols found in the zodiac. For example:

> *Rev 5:5-6a*
> *5 But one of the elders said to me, "Do not weep. Behold, **the Lion** of the tribe of Judah, the Root of David, has prevailed to open the scroll and to loose its seven seals." 6 And I looked, and behold, in the midst of the throne and of the four living creatures, and in the midst of the elders, stood **a Lamb** as though it had been slain, having seven horns and seven eyes...*

The "Lamb" is called "the Lion of the tribe of Judah." From this passage we learn that Aries (the Lamb – the New Covenant sacrifice) is also Leo (the Lion – the King who will reign upon the Throne of David). That the Bible uses the same pictorial language as the ancient constellations is significant evidence that the words of the prophets come from the same source as the signs of the zodiac. Since the signs foretell the same events in the same sequence as the Bible, using the same symbols, a common source is strongly implied.

The parallels between the zodiac and the Bible provide significant circumstantial evidence that both sprang from the same source, or that one borrows significantly from the other. The question that must be resolved, however, is whether the Bible borrows from pagan sources, as is frequently charged by skeptics and atheists, or whether paganism is a corruption of ancient prophecy contained in the constellations from the same God who gave us the Bible, as was claimed by the

MYSTERY of the MAZZAROTH

Apostle Paul. The answer to this question has staggering consequences.

Christians need only show that both the zodiac and the Bible tell the same story in the same sequence, and that the prophecy contained in both is supernatural in nature. The supernatural quality of accurate predictive prophecy requires a Divine source. The story of human history was known and recorded in advance in the pictures of the zodiac as well as the sayings of the Hebrew prophets. No amount of human divination could tell the story of Israel in advance.

Some have tried to counterfeit predictive prophecy. But, their prophecies have either failed totally, or been so vague that they are virtually self-fulfilling. Who but the Creator could write human history in advance across the vastness of the heavens? Who but the Creator could accurately reveal history in advance through a series of prophets? Only the Creator of heaven and earth, who is Himself guiding history, can do such things.

The message of the zodiac and the prophets is supernatural. It identifies the Creator as the God who revealed Himself to Abraham and through the Hebrew prophets. The zodiac identifies Jesus Christ as the Messiah of Israel because it does not end with the Old Testament, but contains the New Testament story as well.

God does not ask that anyone believe and obey Him based upon blind faith. He has revealed Himself clearly for anyone who is truly seeking Him with a sincere and pure heart.

History and the heavens are His witnesses. He has laid out the story of the entire Bible in sequential pictures across the heavens before any of it was history! If this does not impress the skeptic, nothing will.

What God has done ought to inspire in the Christian a deep love for stargazing, and a desire to learn how to identify the constellations in the night sky. Once learned, this ancient form of communication can be used to pass on the knowledge of God to the next generation, just as the sons of Seth did with their children. There is no greater gift one can give his children than knowledge of God through His revelation, including the Mazzaroth — God's prophecy in the constellations.

MYSTERY of the MAZZAROTH

Chapter 2
Ancient Sources

From an archeological perspective, the zodiac has been traced as far back as human civilization itself. It existed in the Sumerian culture, the oldest known civilization. The Sumerians lived in the area of Iraq, between the Tigress and Euphrates rivers where the Tower of Babel once stood. Abraham's hometown, Ur, was a Sumerian city. The only surviving Sumerian archeological evidences of zodiac signs are pictorial representations on cylinder seals and boundary stones.

The Sumerian civilization was eventually replaced by the Babylonians. Evidence from this period consists of the "Three Stars Each" catalogues from the 12th century BC, a tripartite division of the heavens which predicts the seasons for farming purposes. Another important Babylonian artifact is the Mul Apin, a pair of stone tablets from the 10th century BC mentioning all twelve zodiacal constellations.

The greatest volume of evidence for the zodiac comes from the Greeks. This includes statues, painted pottery, and poetry. Aratus' *Phaenomena*, which Paul quoted, is one such Greek source.

The Egyptian zodiac of Dendera is perhaps the most valuable and controversial relic of archeo-astronomy ever discovered, being the oldest surviving circular zodiac. It was removed from the ceiling of the chapel of Osiris in the Egyptian Temple of Hathor in 1821, sold to the French government, and is currently on display at the Louvre in Paris. It contains the same twelve zodiac signs still recognized today. The drawing below was commissioned by Napoleon, and published prior to the zodiac's removal from the temple of Hathor.

Zodiac of Dendera [31]

---

[31] From Description de l' Egypte Antiquites, v. 4.

MYSTERY of the MAZZAROTH

The Dendera zodiac became the subject of heated controversy in France in the 19th century. Claims and counter-claims were made about its antiquity driven by opposite agendas, both Christian and anti-Christian. Some claimed it was many thousands of years older than the Biblical account of creation, thereby casting doubt on the Genesis account. Others claimed it was made no later than 2,000 BC. Still others claimed it was made during the Greco-Roman era, no older than the first century BC.

This later claim was not based on astronomical information derived from the zodiac, but on hieroglyphic inscriptions near the zodiac contained in the drawing reproduced in *Description de l' Egypte Antiquites*. It was later discovered, however, that these inscriptions were added by the printer, and were not actually part of the relic itself.[32]

The modern secular consensus is that the Dendera zodiac was made about 50 BC; it was not intended to depict any particular date or historical event;[33] and the Egyptians borrowed the twelve signs of the zodiac from Greco-Roman sources. However, John H. Rogers pointed out that *"the zodiacal constellations are not shown in their Graeco-Roman forms;*

---

[32] Buchwald, Jed C, Egyptian Stars Under Paris Skies, Engineering and Science, #4, 2003, p. 20, Caltech. http://eands.caltech.edu/articles/Buchwald%20Feature.pdf

[33] The Louvre webpage on the Dendera zodiac claims the positions of the planets date it between June 15 and August 15, AD 50. This claim, however, is false. The planets as they appear in the zodiac cannot indicate any date at all because Mercury is in Virgo and Venus is in Pisces. These are about 180 degrees apart. Yet, Mercury and Venus can never be seen more than 40 degrees apart from each other because of their close proximity to the sun. The planets in the Dendera zodiac are all in their astrological signs of exaltation: Mercury in Virgo, Venus in Pisces, Mars in Capricorn, Jupiter in Cancer, and Saturn in Libra.

MYSTERY of the MAZZAROTH

the shapes of the figures on the Seleucid and Dendera zodiacs are almost identical to each other and to the boundary-stone pictographs from the second millennium BC. So the Dendera zodiac seems to be a complete copy of the Mesopotamian zodiac."[34]

The Dendera zodiac was first assumed to reflect the sky as it existed at the time the temple was erected. However, there is ample evidence that the temple was a reconstruction of a much older Temple on the same site. The zodiac could have been salvaged from an older temple, it could be a copy of an earlier zodiac as Rogers claims, or it could have been intended to depict the sky at an important historical event.

One fact is undeniable: The alignment of the zodiac signs with the solstices and equinoxes in the Dendera zodiac depict the sky as it appeared around 2,300 BC. Due to precession, the solstices and equinoxes are slowly moving through the zodiac, regressing about 1 degree every 72 years, averaging 1 constellation per 2,150 years.[35] Precession is the apparent very slow drifting of the constellations of the zodiac relative to the seasonal markers – the fall and spring equinoxes (when days and nights are exactly the same) and the winter and summer solstices (the longest and shortest days of the year). It is caused by a wobble in the tilted axis of the earth, similar to a wobble of a top when it spins. Our solar calendar is fixed to the seasons so that the equinoxes and solstices fall on about the same specific dates each year on our solar calendar. Our

---

[34] Rogers, John H., Origins of the Ancient Constellations, p. 10, British Astronomical Association

[35] Insofar as the ancients sometimes depicted the solstices and equinoxes as aligning with certain constellations, we are able to approximately date their work.

calendar is locked to the seasons because they have a direct impact on our lives. The positions of the stars do not affect us greatly, so it is of little consequence to our daily lives if the constellations drift slightly over time.

Due to precession, there is a very slow shift between our solar year and what is called the sidereal year. This is the time it takes for our earth to make one revolution around the sun and return to the exact same spot in relation to the background stars. The very small difference between our solar year and the sidereal year means that each year on the same date the constellations will have shifted ever so slightly.

The Dendera zodiac depicts the two solstices and two equinoxes[36] as four images of Hathor (Isis) holding up the hemisphere of the sky at the corners. The summer solstice is aligned with Leo, close to Cancer. The winter solstice is in Aquarius. The spring equinox is in Taurus, close to Aries. The fall equinox is in Libra, close to Scorpio. This configuration depicts the skies around 2,300 BC.

The Dendera zodiac was also surrounded by very large areas of parallel zigzag lines – the Egyptian symbol for water. These lines run the full length of the zodiac. The Dendera zodiac appears to represent the skies above a flooded earth. The center of the zodiac depicts the celestial North Pole, and the

---

[36] The 'solstice' occurs when the sun reaches its highest point in the sky at noon (summer) or lowest (winter) position in the sky at noon (as viewed in the northern hemisphere above the tropic of cancer). At the summer solstice, the days are longest. At the winter solstice, the days are shortest. An "equinox" occurs half way between the solstices, when the sun rises and sets exactly due east and west, and when the days and nights are equal lengths.

outer circle depicts the horizon. There is no representation of the earth at all, only the hemisphere of the sky with nothing but water below the horizon.

Ancient Egyptian creation myths claimed that the earth arose out of a watery chaos following a great cataclysm: *"The Egyptian creation myth is geocentric. Its starting point is a pre-existent proto-earth – a living being of body and soul – which has 'died' following an ill-defined, violent event. ... the proto-earth gathers itself together, rises up from the watery abyss, splits open, and ejects the primeval matter from which the sky-ocean, the stars, the Sun, and the Moon will be born. This is the myth of the separation of the heavens from the earth. Note that the separation takes the form of a cataclysm."*[37]

The Egyptian creation myth did not begin "in the beginning," but rather focused on a rebirth of the earth from a watery grave. This has striking parallels with the biblical story of Noah. It is highly probable that the cataclysm they envisioned was indeed the great flood. The Egyptian myths about the recreation of the earth from a watery abyss were simply their descriptions of the post flood earth and the establishment of the Egyptian civilization afterwards.

It is striking that the Dendera zodiac depicts a date of about 2,300 BC by the alignment of the solstices and equinoxes with the zodiac signs. Noah's flood was also about 2,300 BC—according to biblical chronology. This seems too much of a coincidence to be ignored. No wonder this discovery was so

---

[37] Alford, Alan F., http://www.eridu.co.uk/Author/myth_religion/egyptian.html

controversial and this date so strongly opposed in 19th century France, the epicenter of materialistic atheism.

Perversion of the Zodiac by Pagans

If the signs of the zodiac were marked out by God, and given to Adam's descendants as mnemonic devices for an oral prophecy, that story and its related symbols would have been passed down by Noah to his descendants. This oral tradition must have been capable of telling the divine story independent of later sources, including the Torah, because it preceded written revelation. When God confounded the languages at the Tower of Babel, the various people groups would have carried these prophetic symbols with them. We would expect that the symbols and even elements of the original story would have survived in the many pagan cultures that resulted by isolating these various language groups.

If we consider that since the beginning of time men understood the zodiac to be prophetic, telling the divine story in advance, it is very easy to explain how it came to be used for astrology. The idea of "fate," which underlies astrology and horoscopes, is a perversion of the notion that God Almighty has foretold and foreordained the course of human history and embedded His plan in symbols across the sky. As the true message became increasingly corrupted, astrologers who claimed to have hidden knowledge of the cosmos began to use the heavens in a perverted way. They claimed the private ability to predict the fate of kingdoms, kings, and eventually individuals, in order to make a name for themselves and gain power over people. The tower of Babel was constructed for the purpose of divining the signs of the heavens in order to give the prognosticators power over the masses. *"And they said, 'Come, let us build ourselves a city, and a tower whose top is in [or "for"] the heavens; let us make a name for ourselves, lest we be scattered abroad over the face of the whole earth.' But the LORD came down to see the city and the tower which the sons of men had built."*[38]

Those who pervert religion use it to captivate the minds of men, making them slaves to an elite group. They then use this power for their own advantage and agenda. This has been true in pagan mystery religions, Judaism, Catholicism, Islam, Protestantism, the Occult, cults, and modern astrology.

The Correct Starting Point

The twelve constellations of the zodiac form a continuous circle around the earth. They rise one after the other in the east, moving across the sky from left to right (in the northern hemisphere when facing south) and set in the west. They are therefore read right to left (as is the Hebrew language). Because they form a continuous circle, we need to know where to begin.

Many have concluded that the Sphinx in Giza, Egypt, just east of the Great Pyramid, was intended to indicate the beginning and ending point of the zodiac. The sphinx has the body of a lion and a human head without the traditional Egyptian beard, possibly of a woman. The lion's body is to the west, and the human head is to the east. In the zodiac, the body of

---

[38] Gen 11:4-5

MYSTERY of the MAZZAROTH

Leo is to the celestial west, and the head of Virgo is to the celestial east. The sphinx is perfectly oriented to the ecliptic at noon and midnight on the solstices, and at sunset and sunrise on the equinoxes. This configuration makes the sphinx a perfect indicator of the point of beginning and ending of the zodiac. Whether that was its intent, we can only guess.

Precession provides another possible clue as to where to break into the circle of the zodiac. When we reverse the precession of the equinoxes and solstices to between 4000 – 3950 BC (the time of creation, according to the Bible), the winter solstice is perfectly centered between Leo and Virgo and the ecliptic runs directly through Regulus, the brightest star in Leo. It would take another 26,000 years for these two alignments to occur again. This may imply that precession is a divine clock with a specific starting point.

While the above two possibilities are intriguing and perhaps substantial, we need a more concrete indicator for the beginning point of the zodiac, and the story that it tells. For our purposes, the obvious place to begin is on the first day of creation where the biblical calendar begins. The Jewish new year is called Rosh Hashanah (meaning "head of the year"), beginning at sunset when the new moon is first observed between September 5th and October 5th. This is the anniversary of the first day of creation.

The Jewish calendar combines two calendars, having two new years' days six months apart. The civil calendar is the older calendar, beginning on Rosh Hashanah. However, at the time of the Jews' exodus from Egypt, God told Moses to keep a second sacred calendar that begins in the spring, the month the exodus occurred.[39] The new calendar was to be used for calculating God's festivals. The original calendar continued to be used to calculate the agricultural cycle. Both calendars are still in use today, with their respective new years' days being six months apart. Since the festival calendar was not introduced until the time of the exodus, all of the biblical dates and ages of the sons of Adam, from Seth to Abraham, use the original civil calendar, counting from Rosh Hashanah in the fall. We should begin reading the zodiac with Virgo, because the sun is in Virgo on Rosh Hashanah,[40] New Year's Day on the original calendar.

---

[39] Exodus 12:2

[40] Virgo is also the largest of the constellations within the zodiac. It takes exactly seven weeks (49 days) for the sun to pass through Virgo. The period of seven weeks is very significant in the Law of Moses. Pentecost is the "feast of (7) weeks" (Leviticus 23). And the Jubilee year of release was at the end of seven "weeks" of years (Leviticus 25).

Chapter 3
Virgo
The Abrahamic Covenant

Revelation 12:1-5,14
1 Now a great sign appeared in heaven: a woman clothed with the sun, with the moon under her feet, and on her head a garland of twelve stars. 2 Then being with child, she cried out in labor and in pain to give birth.
3 And another sign appeared in heaven: behold, a great, fiery red dragon having seven heads and ten horns, and seven diadems on his heads. 4 His tail drew a third of the stars of heaven and threw them to the earth. And the dragon stood

before the woman who was ready to give birth, to devour her Child as soon as it was born. 5 She bore a male Child who was to rule all nations with a rod of iron. And her Child was caught up to God and His throne. ...

14 But the woman was given two wings of a great eagle, that she might fly into the wilderness to her place, where she is nourished for a time and times and half a time, from the presence of the serpent.

The Greeks referred to this constellation as "parthenos," meaning "the virgin." The Roman name "virgo" appears to have been borrowed from the Greek. However, "virginity" had no significance whatever in the mythologies associated with Virgo, but rather fertility. A virgin was a woman available for marriage and procreation. Her value was seen in her potential to produce many offspring. A more mature woman who had ceased bearing children had lesser value in ancient cultures. While it is true that a virgin was supposed to be untouched by a male, the term spoke more to her potential fertility than to her past sexuality.

Referring to this constellation as the "virgin" was also a late adaptation. The earliest (Sumerian) name, found in the Babylonian MUL-APIN tablet, was "AB.SIN,"[41] meaning "seed furrow."[42] The emphasis of this constellation was fertility, represented by the sheaf of wheat in her left hand.

---

[41] MUL-APIN 6, Day Differences Rising and Setting Stars, http://www.lexiline.com/lexiline/lexi178.htm

[42] Foxvog, Daniel A, Elementary Sumerian Glossary, p. 4, http://www.anelanguages.com/SumerianGlossaryFoxvog.pdf

MYSTERY of the MAZZAROTH

The brightest star, Spica, means "ear of grain" and is located in the left hand of Virgo.

The figure of a woman holding a sheaf of wheat is an allegory representing female fertility. The act of intercourse was parallel to the planting of wheat, with the husband planting his "seed" in the "furrow" of the woman. Many ancient languages, including the biblical languages, used the same word "seed" for both crops and human procreation. The very first prophecy in Scripture dealt with "the seed of the woman" crushing the head of the serpent.

When a virgin married, the greatest concern of both family and friends was that she would be fertile and produce many children. Infertility was considered a curse. This is illustrated in the biblical account of the competition between Jacob's wives to produce children and the ancient practice of using surrogate wives called concubines. The ritual of throwing grain at a bride and groom is still practiced today. Grain has always been a symbol of fertility. This custom was an allegorical way of saying, "May she be fertile and have many children." The woman represented by Virgo holding a sheaf of wheat does not symbolize virginity, but fertility. She represents the mother of a multitude of offspring.

John's Vision of the Woman Clothed with the Sun
In Revelation 12, the sign in heaven of the woman in labor giving birth to the male child represents the birth of Jesus. John saw the constellation Virgo "in heaven." He located two heavenly bodies – the sun and the moon – relative to her. Virgo is the only woman in the zodiac, and she is

accompanied by the serpent both in John's vision and in the zodiac. The serpent (Hydra) runs parallel to the ecliptic just below Virgo and Leo.

The first piece of information John gave was that she was "clothed with the sun." Throughout the twelve months of the year, the sun slowly moves through all twelve constellations. When the sun is in a particular constellation, that constellation is "clothed with the sun." The constellation is "clothed," as opposed to "naked," because it cannot be seen from the earth's surface due to sunlight illuminating our atmosphere, obscuring the stars. The only time a constellation can be seen from earth when the sun is in that constellation is during a total solar eclipse. Otherwise, the position of the sun in a constellation was determined by observing the constellations opposite it during the night, and calculating its position during the day based on star charts. The ancients devised star maps and precise calculations for determining the sun's position in the houses of the zodiac. With modern computer astronomy programs, the atmosphere can be turned off and the sun's precise position in the zodiac can be observed at any time. Virgo is "clothed with the sun" in September, although the sun's stay in Virgo is slowly changing due to precession. In the centuries around when Jesus was born, the sun was in Virgo from about August 25th to October 10th. The sun was mid-body in Virgo (womb area) between September 10th and September 20th. John's statement that the woman was "clothed with the sun" when she gave birth indicates that the Messiah was born around mid-September.

John said that she wore a garland of twelve stars on her head. Virgo is in a lying down position along the ecliptic. Immediately north (above) Virgo's head is a small constellation called Coma Berenices. This constellation was not part of the original zodiac, but was first conceived by the Egyptians around 243 BC,[43] and was well-known and associated with Virgo when John wrote Revelation. Coma Berenices consists of about ten to fourteen stars that are visible to the naked eye.[44] One of the two brightest stars in this small constellation is "Diadem" – the Greek word for "crown."

John also saw the moon beneath her feet when she gave birth to the Messiah. It takes a year for the sun to slowly pass through all twelve constellations and arrive back at the starting point, but the moon moves much quicker through the constellations, taking only a month to pass through all twelve.

Think of the circle of zodiac signs as the numbers 1-12 on a clock. Number "12" represents the Hebrew month Tishri, which is the first month on the Hebrew calendar (when the sun is in Virgo). This is roughly September on our calendar. The remaining numbers represent the other eleven months of

---

[43] In 243 BC, Ptolemy's new wife, Berenice, swore to Aphrodite that she would sacrifice all her long hair if her husband was granted a safe return from battle. After his return, Berenice fulfilled her vow, cutting off all her hair and placing it in the temple of Aphrodite. But her hair was stolen that very night, and the king became furious. To appease the king, the court astronomer declared that Aphrodite had placed Berenices hair in the sky, as a cluster of stars above the head of Virgo. (Gaius Julius Hyginus, 2:24, Astronomica). Aphrodite was the goddess of motherhood, the Greek equivalent to the Egyptian Isis (Hathor), mother of Horus, whom the Egyptians associated with the constellation Virgo.

[44] 1-5 magnitude

the Hebrew calendar and their corresponding zodiac signs. The sun's cycle through the zodiac is like the slow hour-hand on this imaginary clock, taking a full year to pass through the whole circle. The moon's cycle is like the much quicker minute hand, completing the circle every month. Each minute-mark corresponds to one day or one night, alternating, so the sixty minutes on our clock represent thirty days plus thirty nights alternating during the month. After the minute hand (moon) passes the hour hand (sun), the new month begins. Another new month begins every time the big hand (moon) passes 12, and the hour-hand indicates the month. Thus, the positions of the sun and moon against the constellations tell us both the month and the day of the month.[45]

On Jesus' birthday, the sun was in the midst of Virgo (number "12" on our imaginary clock), which indicates the month was Tishri (September). The moon was beneath her feet (just past 12) indicating the first day of the month. This is Rosh Hashanah,[46] the anniversary of the first day of creation on the Jewish calendar. The alignment of the sun and moon in Virgo, which John described, happens only once a year, on Rosh Hashanah. The Creator stepped into His creation on the anniversary of the creation! Jesus' birthday is not December

---

[45] The moon must pass the sun by about 15 degrees in order for the sliver of the new moon to be visible to the eye after sunset, which is the way the ancients marked the beginning of the month. In the diagram above, the moon has past the sun (both moving counter-clockwise) just enough for the sliver of reflected light to be seen from earth. This marks the "new moon," and the beginning of the month. When this occurs in September, it begins the new year – Rosh Hashanah.

[46] Martin, Dr. Ernest L, The Star that Astonished the World, ch. 5. http://www.askelm.com/star/star006.htm

25th, but Rosh Hashanah, the day beginning at sunset when the new moon is first seen in September.⁴⁷

At dawn on September 12, 3 BC, Rosh Hashanah, the "Bright and Morning Star" (Venus) rose first in the middle of Virgo's head,⁴⁸ being the brightest thing in the sky just before dawn. Jesus called Himself, *"the Offspring of David, the Bright and Morning Star."*⁴⁹ "Offspring" refers to His birth, and "Bright

---

⁴⁷ December 25th is the first day when it becomes apparent that the sun has reversed its southerly retreat in winter and has begun to turn back north to bring its warmth. It is also the first sign that the days have stopped getting shorter and are beginning to get longer. Pagan sun worshippers were afraid that the sun would keep moving south until it disappeared altogether. So, when it became evident that the sun had reversed course, there was cause for celebration. Consequently, they made December 25th the "birthday" of their sun god. This holiday was later adopted by Catholicism as Jesus' birthday in their attempt to assimilate new pagan converts into the church.
⁴⁸ While each Rosh Hashanah the sun was in the midst of Virgo, and the moon under her feet, Venus only appears in her crown very rarely on this date.
⁴⁹ Rev. 22:16

and Morning Star" refers to Venus. Why would Jesus refer to Himself as Venus? The answer is only obvious when we understand the significance of the zodiac in light of Revelation 12. The dawn of Venus in the crown of Virgo on Jesus' birthday represented the birth of the "Man Child."

Some might assume that the woman in John's vision (Virgo) represents Mary since she gave birth to Jesus. However, the zodiac tells the story of the history of God's redemption of His creation, beginning with the call of Abraham and ending with Jesus reigning in His Kingdom. Thus, we would expect Virgo to be related to the beginning of this story – the Abrahamic Covenant. Also, John informs us that the serpent (Hydra) attempts to destroy "the remnants of her offspring"[50] – the faithful believers living during the time of the great tribulation. Christians are not the offspring of Mary.

The serpent is present in John's vision, in the Genesis prophecy, and in the constellations. He is stretched out along the ecliptic just below Virgo and Leo. His Latin name is Hydra, meaning "sea serpent." The serpent, Hydra, ties together the beginning and end of the zodiac cycle (Virgo and Leo), the beginning and end of the story of the redemption of the creation.

---

[50] Rev. 12:17

MYSTERY of the MAZZAROTH

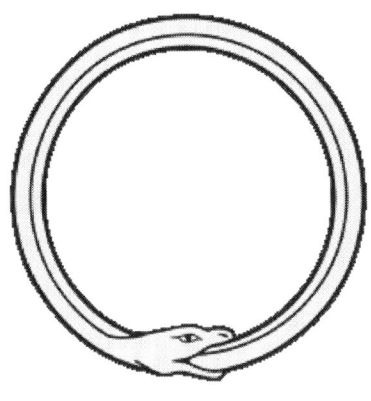

The Ouroboros was an ancient Egyptian symbol of a snake swallowing its tail, as a symbol of cyclicality. It was associated with the beginning and end of the year. The fact that Hydra runs beneath Leo and Virgo, connecting them together, strongly suggests that the ancient Egyptians believed that the year ends as the sun leaves Leo (in August) and begins as the sun enters Virgo (September).

Hydra was a multi-headed sea monster in Greek and Roman mythology. According to some sources he had seven heads; others indicate nine heads; others have fifty or a hundred. The multi-headed sea serpent, seeking to devour the man child in Revelation 12, and then persecuting the woman and her seed, is unquestionably Satan. At the end of the story, the serpent is destroyed by Leo (the lion), and the repeating yearly cycle of the zodiac comes to an end.

In the Dendera zodiac, Leo is pictured standing on the serpent, Hydra, showing his victory over him. Satan's dominion will end by the hand of the man child, the Lion of the tribe of Judah.

Virgo Represents Sarah, Abraham's Wife

The very first prophecy in Scripture of the coming Messiah is found in Genesis 3:15 and it was spoken by God to the Serpent. *"And I will put enmity between you and the woman, and between your seed and her Seed; He shall bruise your head, and you shall bruise His heel."* The promised "Seed" of the woman is Jesus Christ, the "male Child" of John's vision. In the above passage, we might be tempted to suppose that the "woman" is Eve. Certainly Eve and Mary are both mothers of Jesus Christ, both appearing in His genealogy. But there is another mother in the lineage of the Messiah who is not only the mother of Jesus but also the mother of all who are *"Abraham's seed and heirs according to the promises."*[51] Her name is Sarah, Abraham's wife. That Sarah is the mother of both the Redeemer and all the redeemed is stated plainly in Scripture. The covenant God made with Abraham concerned both a nation and a single individual.

> *Gen 15:2-5*
> *2 But Abram said, "Lord GOD, what will You give me, seeing I go childless, and the heir of my house is Eliezer of Damascus?" 3 Then Abram said, "Look, You have given me no offspring; indeed one born in my house is my heir!"*
> *4 And behold, the word of the LORD came to him, saying, "This one shall not be your heir, but one who will come from your own body shall be your heir." 5 Then He brought him outside and said, "Look now toward heaven, and count the stars if you are able to number them." And He said to him, "So shall your descendants be."*

---

[51] Galatians 3:29

Abraham's attention was directed by God to the stars to behold what God was going to do. Yet, God's promise was not limited to the nation of Israel. Through Abraham all nations would be blessed. Abraham would become the father of "many nations." The innumerable stars in the sky were likened to Abraham's seed. He is the father of all the redeemed because he is the father of Jesus Christ.

> *Gen. 17:4-5*
> *4 "As for Me, behold, My covenant is with you, and you shall be a father of many nations. 5 No longer shall your name be called Abram, but your name shall be Abraham; for I have made you a father of many nations.*

The Apostle Paul interpreted God's promise as referring explicitly to Jesus Christ, the particular descendant of Abraham through whom all the nations would be blessed.

> *Gal. 3:16, 26-29*
> *16 Now to Abraham and his Seed were the promises made. He does not say, "And to seeds," [plural] as of many, but as of one, "And to your Seed," [singular] who is Christ. ...*
> *26 For you are all sons of God through faith in Christ Jesus. 27 For as many of you as were baptized into Christ have put on Christ. 28 There is neither Jew nor Greek, there is neither slave nor free, there is neither male nor female; for you are all one in Christ Jesus. 29 And if you are Christ's, then you are Abraham's seed, and heirs according to the promise.*

Here, Paul appealed to the grammar contained in the original promise. He noted that "seed" was singular, not plural. The promise he quoted from Genesis referred to one of Abraham's descendants whom he identified as "Christ." Paul then concluded that those who have been placed "in Christ" through baptism are "Abraham's seed" (because Christ is Abraham's seed) and consequently are legitimate heirs to the inheritance promised to Jesus Christ – Abraham's Seed. That inheritance is the land God promised to Abraham and his "Seed" as an everlasting possession.

The clause, "and to your Seed," (και τω σπερματι σου) was quoted verbatim by Paul from the Septuagint version of Genesis 13:17. It appears again in Gen. 17:8. In both passages the eternal land inheritance is in view. These are the only two verses relating to Abraham which contain the clause Paul quoted in Galatians 3, (και τω σπερματι σου).

> *Gen 13:17 LXX*
> 17 *Arise and traverse* **the land**, *both in the length of it and in the breadth; for to thee will I give it,* **and to thy seed** [και τω σπερματι σου] *forever.*
>
> *Gen. 17:8 LXX*
> 8 *And I will give to thee* **and to thy seed** [και τω σπερματι σου] *after thee* **the land** *wherein thou sojournest, even all the land of Chanaan for an everlasting possession, and I will be to them a God.*

The land inheritance is Christ's own inheritance, and those who are in Him.[52] The Promised Land, in which Abraham

---

[52] Hebrews 1:1-3 & 2:10

dwelled in tents with Isaac and Jacob as foreigners, is the land that Jesus Christ will restore and inherit along with the children of God: *"and if children, then heirs — heirs of God and joint heirs with Christ, if indeed we suffer with Him, that we may also be glorified together."*[53]

In Galatians 4, the Apostle Paul explained that Sarah is the mother of all the redeemed.

> *Gal 4:21-31*
> *21 Tell me, you who desire to be under the law, do you not hear the law?*
> *22 For it is written that Abraham had two sons: the one by a bondwoman, the other by **a freewoman**.*
> *23 But he who was of the bondwoman was born according to the flesh, and he of **the freewoman** through promise,*
> *24 which things are symbolic. For these are the two covenants: the one from Mount Sinai which gives birth to bondage, which is Hagar —*
> *25 for this Hagar is Mount Sinai in Arabia, and corresponds to Jerusalem which now is, and is in bondage with her children —*
> *26 but **the Jerusalem above is free, which is the mother of us all**.*
> *27 For it is written: "Rejoice, O barren, You who do not bear! Break forth and shout, You who are not in labor! For the desolate has many more children Than she who has a husband."*

---

[53] Romans 8:17

> 28 _Now we, brethren, as Isaac was, are children of promise_.
> 29 But, as he who was born according to the flesh then persecuted him who was born according to the Spirit, even so it is now.
> 30 Nevertheless what does the Scripture say? "Cast out the bondwoman and her son, for the son of the bondwoman shall not be heir with the son of **the freewoman**."
> 31 So then, brethren, _we are not children of the bondwoman but of the free_.

Sarah was the physical mother of the nation of Israel. More importantly, she was the mother of Jesus Christ because He was the very "Seed" (singular) of Abraham and Sarah to whom the promises were made, tracing His lineage back through Mary, David, Judah, Jacob, Isaac, and Abraham. As Paul explained in Galatians 3, those who are baptized into Jesus Christ become *"Abraham's seed and heirs according to the promise"* because they are joined to Jesus Christ, the "Seed" of the promise. True Christians are children of the freewoman, Sarah. She is the mother of both the Redeemer and the redeemed.

Sarah, the Inspiration for the Egyptian, Isis (Hathor)

Virgo is depicted in ancient astrological drawings and writings as holding a sheaf of wheat in her left hand and a branch in her right hand. In Egyptian mythology, Virgo scattered the wheat grain, which then became the Milky Way. *"For Egyptians she [Virgo] was associated with the goddess Isis, portrayed with wheat in her hand. It is said that when the monster*

Typhon pursued her, she dropped the sheaf, scattering wheat across the sky to become the glittering Milky Way."[54]

Because of the famine in Canaan, Abraham went down to Egypt after God had promised to give the land to him and his descendants forever. We are told in Genesis 12 that Sarah was a very beautiful woman, so much so that Abraham feared he would be killed by the Egyptians and his wife stolen from him. So Abraham conspired with Sarah to say only that she was his sister. Pharaoh, (who was considered a god), was so taken with Sarah's beauty, he attempted to add her to his harem. *"But the LORD plagued Pharaoh and his house with great plagues because of Sarai, Abram's wife."*[55]

Josephus cited the third century BC Babylonian astronomer, Berossus, who wrote of Abraham's skill in astronomy. *"Berosus mentions our father Abram without naming him, when he says thus: 'In the tenth generation after the Flood, there was among the Chaldeans a man righteous and great, and skillful in the celestial science'."*[56] Josephus went on to say that Abraham was the source of the Egyptians' knowledge of astronomy. *"He communicated to them arithmetic, and delivered to them the science of astronomy; for before Abram came into Egypt they were unacquainted with those parts of learning; for that science came from the Chaldeans into Egypt, and from thence to the Greeks also."*[57]

---

[54] Project Astro Utah, Virgo,
http://www.clarkfoundation.org/astro-utah/vondel/virgo.html
[55] Genesis 12:17
[56] Josephus, Antiquities, Book 1, ch. vii, 2
[57] Josephus, Antiquities, Book I, Ch. viii, 2

It is usually supposed that Egyptian knowledge of the zodiac was borrowed from the Greeks, and hence not as ancient as Babylonian knowledge. However, the zodiac of Dendera used zodiac symbols identical with Sumerian and Babylonian astronomy, which was very different in design from the Greek counterparts. This evidence strongly suggests that the source of the Egyptian knowledge of the zodiac came from Sumerian or Chaldean sources (where Abraham was born) rather than from Greek sources as is often supposed.[58] This evidence supports Josephus' claim.

Abraham and Sarah must have had a huge impact on the Egyptians. Understanding the workings of the heavens was considered divine knowledge by the ancients, as the Book of Enoch[59] illustrates. Abraham's vast knowledge of mathematics and astronomy, which he imparted to the Egyptians, would have given him god-like status with his Egyptian hosts. Sarah's incredible beauty and the supernatural plagues brought upon Pharaoh because of Sarah

---

[58] White, Gavin, Babylonian Star Lore, A New Interpretation of the Dendera Zodiac;
http://www.solaria-ublications.com/a_new_interpretation_of_the_dendera_zodiac
[59] The Book of Enoch is ascribed to Enoch, the great-grandfather of Noah and son of Jared (Genesis 5:18). It is considered pseudepigrapha and non-canonical, written after the Babylonian exile. However, it has great historical value, showing how the Jews after the Babylonian exile understood astronomy. It describes Enoch's being taught the workings of the heavens by angels. Much of it is absurd and scientifically impossible. For example, Enoch was told that the sun is carried through the heavens in a horse drawn chariot. He was told that the sun comes through a window in the eastern horizon each day and exits through a window in the western horizon. It then moves around the earth back to the east by way of the north. He was told that the stars and planets are living creatures. That this information was allegedly delivered to Enoch by angels demonstrates that the ancients considered knowledge of astronomy to be divine knowledge.

would have also elevated her to goddess-like status. If not seen as gods themselves, Abraham and Sarah would certainly be seen as having a unique relationship with the gods, or as messengers of the gods.

The later Egyptian myths of Osiris and Isis (Hathor) are strikingly similar to the biblical account of Abraham and Sarah. God showed Abraham the Milky Way, and promised him that His descendants through Sarah would be "as the stars of heaven." The Egyptians, in their worship of Isis, depicted her as scattering her grain to form the innumerable stars of the Milky Way—Abraham's promised seed.

Isis was both the wife and sister of Osiris in Egyptian mythology; Sarah was both the wife and sister of Abraham.[60] Isis was the mother of Horus, who was said to have been conceived supernaturally. The conception of Isaac was a miracle. Isis was considered the goddess of fertility. It was through Sarah that Abraham would become "the father of many nations," a promise consistently interpreted in the New Testament as referring to Christians.[61]

The Egyptians already had a myth regarding the constellation Virgo (Isis / Hathor) when Abraham and Sarah arrived, perhaps a perverted remnant of an oral tradition passed down from Noah. However, it seems highly likely that the Egyptians considered them the personifications of Osiris and Isis, the fulfillment of their mythology, and the prophetic sign of Virgo. Prior to its removal from the Temple of Hathor, the

---

[60] Genesis 20:12
[61] Romans 4:13-17

Dendera zodiac was bordered on one side by a very large image of Hathor (Isis).[62] The constellation Aries is aligned perfectly with Hathor's vaginal area. Aries is the "Lamb of God," Jesus Christ, the "seed of the woman," the "man-child," the singular "Seed" of Abraham through Sarah to whom the promise was made, and through whom it will be realized by all true children of Sarah – all those who are in Christ.

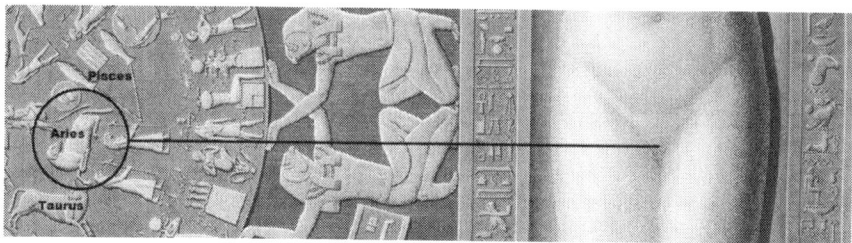

The pagan mythologies were perversions of an original true prophetic message communicated by God to the sons of Seth. The signs of the zodiac were created to be used as mnemonic devices, visual aids to communicate the prophetic story from generation to generation. As a descendant of Seth, Noah preserved these antediluvian prophecies and passed them on through his sons. Yet, man quickly began to corrupt God's truth, creating absurd myths and worshipping the heavenly bodies as gods. After God confounded the languages at the tower of Babel, the various language groups split up, settling in diverse locations. The Egyptians, like all other groups, carried with them oral traditions of corrupt mythologies containing remnants of the original prophecies. The myths surrounding Osiris, Isis, and Horus are no doubt corruptions

---

[62] See full illustration on page 34.

of the original prophecy communicated by God to the ancients and illustrated in the constellation, Virgo.

The Branch in Virgo's Right Hand

Virgo is often depicted as having a small palm branch in her right hand.[63] The branch is a symbol of that one particular "Seed" through whom all the nations would be blessed. We find the same Branch metaphor used of the Messiah throughout biblical prophecy.

> *Isaiah 11:1-2*
> *1 There shall come forth **a Rod** from the stem of Jesse, And **a Branch** shall grow out of his roots. 2 The Spirit of the LORD shall rest upon Him, The Spirit of wisdom and understanding, The Spirit of counsel and might, The Spirit of knowledge and of the fear of the LORD.*

Isaiah's prophecy refers to the Davidic Covenant—that the Messiah would come through David's seed and would sit upon David's throne, reigning over the house of Jacob forever.

Virgo's Wings

Finally, ancient depictions of Virgo often include wings.[64] The purpose of these wings is revealed for us in John's vision of Virgo clothed with the sun. *"But the woman was given two wings of a great eagle, that she might fly into the wilderness to her place, where she is nourished for a time and times and half a time,*

---

[63] See illustration on page 43.
[64] See illustration on page 43.

from the presence of the serpent."[65] During the time of great tribulation yet to come, Abraham's seed will flee to places of safety in the wilderness where God will provide shelter and food. This refers to faithful Christians. Sarah, the "freewoman," is the mother of all who have been redeemed to God through the sacrifice of Jesus Christ. All who have been baptized into Jesus Christ have put on Christ. Christians are, therefore, Abraham's seed and heirs according to the promises to Abraham's seed,[66] including this one.

The two eagle's wings in John's vision are also meant to refer the reader of Revelation back to the time of the exodus as a model for what God will do for His faithful followers in the coming time of great tribulation. God told Israel through Moses, *"You have seen what I did to the Egyptians, and how I bore you on eagles' wings and brought you to Myself."*[67] God's provision of a miraculous escape from Egypt and manna in the wilderness are meant to typify what God will do for faithful believers in the end-time drama. Virgo fled with "eagle's wings" from the serpent (Pharaoh) through the Red Sea into the wilderness. Pharaoh's army was swallowed up in the sea. Virgo will flee again from the serpent (Antichrist) on "eagle's wings" into the wilderness during the end-time drama. Antichrist's army will be swallowed up by the earth.[68]

---

[65] Revelation 12:14
[66] Galatians 3:26-29
[67] Exodus 19:4
[68] Revelation 12:15-16

Chapter 4
Libra
The Law of Moses

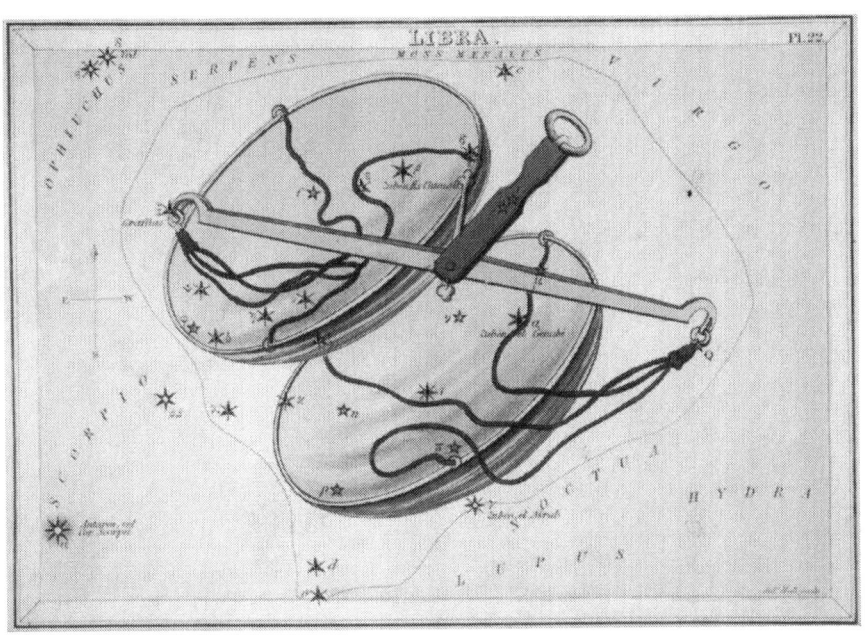

Leviticus 19:35-37
35 "You shall do no injustice in judgment, in measurement of length, weight, or volume.
*36 You shall have **honest scales**, honest weights, an honest ephah, and an honest hin: I am the LORD your God, who brought you out of the land of Egypt.*
37 Therefore you shall observe all My statutes and all My judgments, and perform them: I am the LORD.'"

MYSTERY of the MAZZAROTH

The Greeks apparently combined the scales with Scorpio, making the two scales the claws of the scorpion. Some claim that the Romans invented Libra. However, we find much earlier evidence that the scales were indeed part of the oldest known zodiac—that of the Sumerians. *"According to historian Gwyneth Heuter, the Sumerians knew this area as ZIB-BA AN-NA, the balance of heaven, 2000 years BC. Hence it seems that the Romans revived a constellation that existed before Greek times."*[69] The Babylonian star catalogue, MUL-APIN, dated to about 1200 BC, lists "the scales" in the Sumerian language,[70] demonstrating that this constellation was indeed part of the original zodiac. We also find the scales in the Egyptian zodiac of Dendera, right where it should be, between Virgo and Scorpio.

The constellation Libra brings us to the Law of Moses, given 430 years after God made the covenant with Abraham. The scales represent the justice of the Law. In the tenth chapter of 1 Corinthians, Paul wrote that the experience of the Israelites in the wilderness was for our instruction. He likened the Red Sea crossing to our baptism; he likened their eating manna and drinking from the rock to our Communion; and he

---

[69] Ridpath, Ian, Startales, Libra, http://www.ianridpath.com/startales/libra.htm
[70] Babylonian Star Catalogue, MUL.APIN, "ZIB.BA.AN.NA "The Scales"

likened their wandering in the wilderness to the toils of this present life. The Israelites entering the Promised Land represents our future inheritance in Christ's coming Kingdom. In fact, the whole history of God's dealing with Israel was meant to provide a historical archetype for how God will ultimately deal with all people.

It is significant that God first allowed Abraham's descendants to suffer greatly as slaves in Egypt before finally delivering them from slavery through Moses. The ordeal in Egypt was no accident. God foretold this to Abraham.[71] Given Paul's remark that all things happened to them as examples for us, what was the purpose of their slavery and oppression so soon after God began fulfilling His promise to Abraham? God was teaching His chosen people some critical lessons by experience. While Abraham certainly knew God intimately, there was no guarantee that his descendants would follow in his footsteps. Every generation of Abraham's descendants needed to know this God and understand His character. This was accomplished by God's working out a series of vital lessons through their history, and by His insistence that they commemorate holidays like Passover to instruct their children. These lessons of Israel's unfolding history appear in the constellations.

The first lesson was a demonstration of God's compassion, delivering them from slavery. When God appeared to Moses in the burning bush He said, *"I have surely seen the oppression of My people who are in Egypt, and have heard their cry because of*

---

[71] Genesis 15:13

their taskmasters, for I know their sorrows. So I have come down to deliver them out of the hand of the Egyptians, and to bring them up from that land to a good and large land, to a land flowing with milk and honey, to the place of the Canaanites and the Hittites and the Amorites and the Perizzites and the Hivites and the Jebusites. Now therefore, behold, the cry of the children of Israel has come to Me, and I have also seen the oppression with which the Egyptians oppress them."[72]

Nothing brings a cry for justice more than being oppressed. Forced slavery of human beings is one of the greatest injustices. For the fledgling nation of Israel, this burden of slavery was compounded by Pharaoh's order to kill all the Hebrew infant boys as a means of population control. Moses himself demonstrated this cry for justice by killing an Egyptian taskmaster who was abusing a fellow Hebrew.

God called the Israelites out of the "house of bondage" to reveal Himself to His chosen nation. His love for them was evident in that He delivered them. His power was evident in the manner in which He delivered them: plagues, parting the Red Sea, and when He descended on Mt. Sinai in smoke and fire. Through these demonstrations they learned to fear Him. But fearing God's awesome power was not enough. One can easily fear those who wield great power, but not necessarily respect or love them.

---

[72] Exodus 3:7-9

God's ultimate desire for Israel was a personal relationship, both individually and collectively. By giving Israel His Law, one of God's greatest attributes—justice—was put on display. The Law elevated Israel above the rest of the nations to a higher moral standard. The Law of Moses introduced a new way of life, of governing a nation, ensuring equal justice for all. *"If a man causes disfigurement of his neighbor, as he has done, so shall it be done to him—fracture for fracture, eye for eye, tooth for tooth; as he has caused disfigurement of a man, so shall it be done to him. And whoever kills an animal shall restore it; but whoever kills a man shall be put to death. You shall have the same law for the stranger and for one from your own country; for I am the LORD your God."*[73]

The Law of Moses provided a safety net for the needy. Farmers were instructed not to harvest the corners of their fields. And when the harvesters dropped some of the produce, it was to be left behind for the poor to gather up to feed their families.

Slaves were to be treated with respect and dignity. Slaves could not serve more than seven years. They must be released on the Sabbath year (every 7th year). Property rights were respected, with all land sold reverting back to the original owner in the year of Jubilee.

A legal system was set in place with specific penalties for specific crimes. No one was to be charged with a crime unless there were at least two independent corroborating witnesses.

---

[73] Leviticus 24:19-20

Even the rulers of the people were restricted by the Law of Moses from abusing their power and oppressing the people of God.

The oppression of the Israelites by the Egyptians had caused them to long for relief and justice. And God gave them both, based on His just nature. But they soon discovered that the same Law that brought deliverance to the oppressed and equity in justice also condemned all men as sinners. We all want justice when we have been wronged by someone else, but when we are the guilty party, justice isn't quite as appealing.

All men are sinners and tend to have only their own self-interests at heart. "Equity" in the eyes of individuals tends to be skewed toward self-interest. Thus, the righteous and equitable standard that God required quickly became a burden for the fallen sons of Adam living in a cursed environment. Each man tried to interpret the Law as it would best benefit him. But even with the best intentions, man's nature falls far short of God's justice. The Law was good, but its standards based on God's nature were too high for fallible human beings. Trying to keep the Law in every point became an unbearable load.

The Apostle Paul eventually concluded that the Law of Moses brought to Israel a kind of oppression of its own, similar to what the Israelites felt in Egypt – a "yoke of bondage"[74] which "neither our fathers nor we were able to bear."[75] But God did

---

[74] Galatians 5:1
[75] Acts 15:10

not wish to place a heavy burden on His people needlessly. The Apostle Paul spent considerable space in his epistles to the Romans, Galatians, and Hebrews, discussing God's ultimate goal for giving His Law. *"Now we know that whatever the law says, it says to those who are under the law, that every mouth may be stopped, and all the world may become guilty before God. Therefore by the deeds of the law no flesh will be justified in His sight, for by the law is the knowledge of sin."*[76] *"What purpose then does the law serve? It was added because of transgressions, till the Seed should come to whom the promise was made; and it was appointed through angels by the hand of a mediator."* [77] *"But the Scripture has confined all under sin, that the promise by faith in Jesus Christ might be given to those who believe. But before faith came, we were kept under guard by the law, kept for the faith which would afterward be revealed. Therefore the law was our tutor to bring us to Christ, that we might be justified by faith."*[78]

Israel's slavery in Egypt was intended by God to provoke a cry for justice and relief from oppression by other people. The Law revealed that God is a just God. Slavery created a yearning in their hearts for God's own attribute, justice. Yet, the same Law that defended the innocent and punished the guilty condemns all men. It illustrates that we are slaves to our own sinful human nature and unable to meet God's just standard. Those living under the Law soon realized that they could not measure up. The Law became the source of condemnation and a cruel slave-driver.

---

[76] Romans 3:19
[77] Galatians 3:19
[78] Galatians 3:22-24

This too was God's plan—not to condemn man, but to instruct him so that he might use the gift of free will wisely to his own benefit. Seeing one's true condition in contrast to God's righteous standard is a critical step along the path towards a personal relationship with God. He is ultimately not interested in condemning anyone. As Peter pointed out, the Lord *"is not willing that any should perish, but that all should come to repentance."*[79] He is a God of love and mercy. And the relationship He desires with each person is one that is based on willing, mutual love. Allowing Israel a glimpse of His justice, which quickly revealed their own failures, provided Him with the context in which to demonstrate His greatest attributes—love and mercy. But before love and mercy can be fully appreciated, mankind needs a good dose of humility.

God delivered His Law to Israel knowing that it would condemn them as sinners. Yet, His promise of a Redeemer was made before the Law was given. The Seed of the woman who would crush the serpent's head (the Branch in the right hand of Virgo) provided hope that *"God will provide Himself a Lamb,"*[80] just as He did for Isaac, Sarah's firstborn son. The rituals contained in the Law, particularly the yearly reenacting of the Passover, pointed to the coming *"Lamb of God who takes away the sin of the world."*

> *Exodus 12:3, 5-7, 12-13*
> *3 Speak to all the congregation of Israel, saying: 'On the tenth of this month every man shall take for himself a lamb, according to the house of his father, a lamb for a household...*

---

[79] 2 Peter 3:9
[80] Genesis 22:7-8

5 Your lamb shall be without blemish, a male of the first year. You may take it from the sheep or from the goats.
6 Now you shall keep it until the fourteenth day of the same month. Then the whole assembly of the congregation of Israel shall kill it at twilight.
7 And they shall take some of the blood and put it on the two doorposts and on the lintel of the houses where they eat it. ...
12 For I will pass through the land of Egypt on that night, and will strike all the firstborn in the land of Egypt, both man and beast; and against all the gods of Egypt I will execute judgment: I am the LORD.
13 Now the blood shall be a sign for you on the houses where you are. And when I see the blood, I will pass over you; and the plague shall not be on you to destroy you when I strike the land of Egypt.

All seven of the feasts God commanded Israel to keep in the Law are prophetic of God's redemptive plan – where mercy would eventually trump justice. It is no surprise that the prophetic story told by the feasts is the same as the prophetic story proclaimed in the zodiac. The timing of the feasts corresponds perfectly with the sun's stay in the respective houses of the zodiac, as will be demonstrated.

Slavery and oppression caused the Israelites to cry out for justice. The Law caused them to cry out for mercy. But woven into the very fabric of the Law itself, through the symbolism of the animal sacrifices and within the prophecy of the zodiac, there remained the promise that one day God was going to provide the ultimate sacrifice for sins so that man could be reconciled to God. This compassionate and loving God would do for man what man could not do for himself—relieve him of condemnation.

Chapter 5
Scorpio
The Sting of God's Rejection

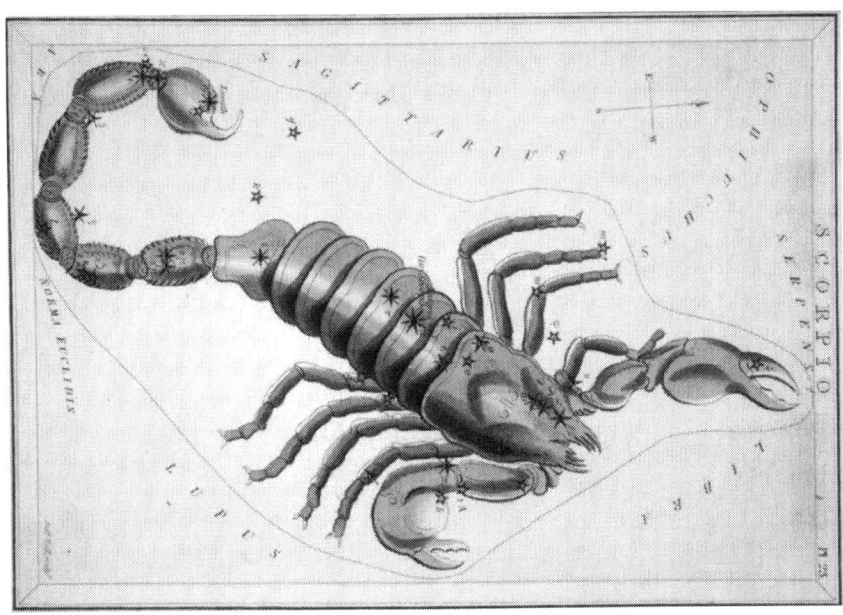

Deuteronomy 8:11-16
11 "Beware that you do not forget the LORD your God by not keeping His commandments, His judgments, and His statutes which I command you today,
12 lest—when you have eaten and are full, and have built beautiful houses and dwell in them;
13 and when your herds and your flocks multiply, and your silver and your gold are multiplied, and all that you have is multiplied;

14 when your heart is lifted up, and you forget the LORD your God who brought you out of the land of Egypt, from the house of bondage;
*15 who led you through that great and terrible wilderness, in which were **fiery serpents and scorpions** and thirsty land where there was no water; who brought water for you out of the flinty rock;*
*16 who fed you in the wilderness with manna, which your fathers did not know, **that He might humble you and that He might test you, to do you good in the end**.*

The simplest explanation for the confusion in the Greek zodiac, combining the claws of the scorpion with the scales, is that these two constellations were connected in their original message. The Law carries with it the penalty for breaking it—the sting of the scorpion. The passage quoted above refers to the Israelites' wilderness experience as characterized by "fiery serpents and scorpions." Indeed, these symbolize the agony Israel felt when they finally got a taste of God's rejection because of their rebellion.

Scorpio brings us to a very dark time in Israel's history. Only a few weeks after God parted the Red Sea and drowned Pharaoh's pursuing army, He appeared to them on Mt. Sinai in a display that struck fear into their hearts. God called Moses up into the mountain and delivered to him the Ten Commandments. Moses was absent from the camp for forty days. During his absence, the Israelites insisted that Aaron make a golden calf. While Moses was in the presence of God receiving the Law, the people were in the camp imitating pagan practices they had seen back in Egypt.

Their rebellion did not end there, despite swift and severe judgment. There was constant complaining about the manna and perceived lack of water. They continually accused Moses of bringing them into the wilderness to let them die of hunger and thirst, claiming that they were better off as slaves in Egypt: at least they had spicy food in Egypt. On more than one occasion God became so angered by their complaining, He told Moses to step aside so He could destroy them all and bring Moses' children into the Promised Land.

This pattern of unbelief and ingratitude came to a head at Kadesh Barnea. God brought them to the border of the Promised Land. Moses sent in twelve spies to gather information useful for battle. Ten of the twelve spies returned with a bad report, claiming that the people were too great for them, and that they would surely be defeated. They did not believe God's promise to go before them into battle. *"And all the children of Israel complained against Moses and Aaron, and the whole congregation said to them, 'If only we had died in the land of Egypt! Or if only we had died in this wilderness! Why has the LORD brought us to this land to fall by the sword, that our wives and children should become victims? Would it not be better for us to return to Egypt?' So they said to one another, "Let us select a leader and return to Egypt."*[81]

God became so furious at their faithlessness and ungrateful attitude that He pronounced upon them the most severe judgment imaginable. Since they did not want to go into the land He promised to give them, they would remain in the

---

[81] Numbers 14:2-4

wilderness for forty years until that whole generation died. God would take their children into the land and give it to them. *"Then the LORD said to Moses: "<u>**How long will these people reject Me**</u>? And how long will they not believe Me, with all the signs which I have performed among them?"*[82]... *"The carcasses of you who have complained against Me shall fall in this wilderness, all of you who were numbered, according to your entire number, from twenty years old and above. ... But your little ones, whom you said would be victims, I will bring in, and they shall know the land which you have despised. But as for you, your carcasses shall fall in this wilderness. And your sons shall be shepherds in the wilderness forty years, and bear the brunt of your infidelity, until your carcasses are consumed in the wilderness. According to the number of the days in which you spied out the land, forty days, for each day you shall bear your guilt one year, namely forty years, and <u>**you shall know My rejection**</u>."*[83]

God's rejection and His withdrawal from them soon began to sting like the scorpion. They begged Him to give them another chance, but it was too late. Their sentence had been passed, and God would not reverse it. They had rejected the God of their forefathers even after He provided continuous miracles and demonstrations of His power and faithfulness to keep His promises. Now God rejected that whole generation. They failed to realize that *"every good gift and every perfect gift is from above, and comes down from the Father of lights, with whom there is no variation or shadow of turning."*[84] How can anyone enjoy good things when he rejects the only source of goodness

---

[82] Numbers 14:11
[83] Numbers 14:29-34
[84] James 1:16-17

— God Himself? God's sentence upon that generation brought the sting of God's rejection. Like the sting of the scorpion, there was no relief. For that generation, all that was left was hell on earth and the realization that the good things God had promised them had been forfeited. This is also the agony that has been and will be endured by those who spurn God's love and goodness by turning their back on Jesus Christ, the ultimate demonstration of God's mercy – His Son, given as a sacrifice for our sins.[85]

When we look at the symbolism of Scripture, it quickly becomes apparent that the scorpion represents the sting of death as the punishment for rebellion against God. Speaking of the resurrection of the body, the ultimate victory over death promised to all who are in Christ, the Apostle Paul pictured death as a scorpion's sting, and linked it to the punishment brought by the Law.

> *1 Cor. 15:54-57*
> *54 So when this corruptible has put on incorruption, and this mortal has put on immortality, then shall be brought to pass the saying that is written: "Death is swallowed up in victory."*
> *55 "O Death, where is your <u>**sting**</u>? O Hades, where is your victory?"*
> *56 <u>**The sting of death is sin, and the strength of sin is the law**</u>.*
> *57 But thanks be to God, who gives us the victory through our Lord Jesus Christ.*

---

[85] Hebrews 6:4-8; 10:26-30

In verse 55, Paul paraphrased Hosea 13:14 (LXX) which first associated the penalty of sin (death) with the sting of the scorpion. *"I will deliver them out of the power of Hades, and will redeem them from death: where is thy penalty, O death? O Hades, where is thy sting?"* Paul then explained that the "sting" found in death is caused by sin. It is sin that brings God's rejection, separating us from all goodness which flows from Him alone. In death, that separation and rejection becomes permanent. Paul then named the source of sin's power—the Law. The righteous standard of the Law, which was based on God's own righteousness, is so far out of our reach that it magnifies our failures and points out how impossible it is to have a relationship with a holy God. When Isaiah got just a glimpse of God, he cried out, *"Woe is me, for I am undone! Because I am a man of unclean lips, And I dwell in the midst of a people of unclean lips; For my eyes have seen the King, The LORD of hosts."*[86]

The agony of God's withdrawing from us when we reject Him is intended to sting. It is not that God wishes to inflict pain upon us. *"'As I live,' says the Lord GOD, 'I have no pleasure in the death of the wicked, but that the wicked turn from his way and live. Turn, turn from your evil ways! For why should you die, O house of Israel?'"*[87] God withdraws from the wicked, and in doing so they suffer the sting of their sin because God is the source of all goodness, light, love, and life. When He withdraws, so also are goodness, light, love, and life withdrawn. People suffer in agony because they have rejected the only source of comfort and all that is good, and the end result is death.

---

[86] Isaiah 6:5
[87] Ezekiel 33:11

Yet even so, God holds out hope that the temporary sting of His rejection will create in the hearts of sinners a deep longing for His refreshing presence, restoration, and reconciliation. It is only when all attempts by God to lead the sinner to repentance have failed that God finally rejects him totally, leaving him to suffer the sting of His rejection in this life, and the ultimate sting of being locked out of His coming Kingdom. The complete absence of God's presence leaves the sinner without the promise of eternal life in the resurrection, leaving only the second death.

> *Luke 13:25-28*
> *25 When once the Master of the house has risen up and shut the door, and you begin to stand outside and knock at the door, saying, 'Lord, Lord, open for us,' and He will answer and say to you, 'I do not know you, where you are from,'*
> *26 then you will begin to say, 'We ate and drank in Your presence, and You taught in our streets.'*
> *27 But He will say, 'I tell you I do not know you, where you are from. Depart from Me, all you workers of iniquity.'*
> *28 There will be weeping and gnashing of teeth, when you see Abraham and Isaac and Jacob and all the prophets in the kingdom of God, and yourselves thrust out.*

Ophiuchus and Serpens

We began this chapter by quoting Deuteronomy 8:11-16. In that passage God spoke to the children of those whom He had brought out from Egypt. The forty years' penalty had passed. The generation which passed through the Red Sea had suffered God's rejection and died in the wilderness. Their children, now grown, were preparing to enter the Promised

Land under the leadership of Joshua. God reminded them that He was the one *"who led you through that great and terrible wilderness, in which were **<u>fiery serpents and scorpions</u>** and thirsty land where there was no water; who brought water for you out of the flinty rock."*[88]

The mention of both serpents and scorpions in this passage is no coincidence. Directly above and overlapping the constellation Scorpio is a constellation called Ophiuchus. The Babylonians included this constellation within the sign of Scorpio as part of their original zodiac. It is sometimes called the thirteenth constellation of the Babylonian zodiac. But in reality, it is a part of Scorpio.

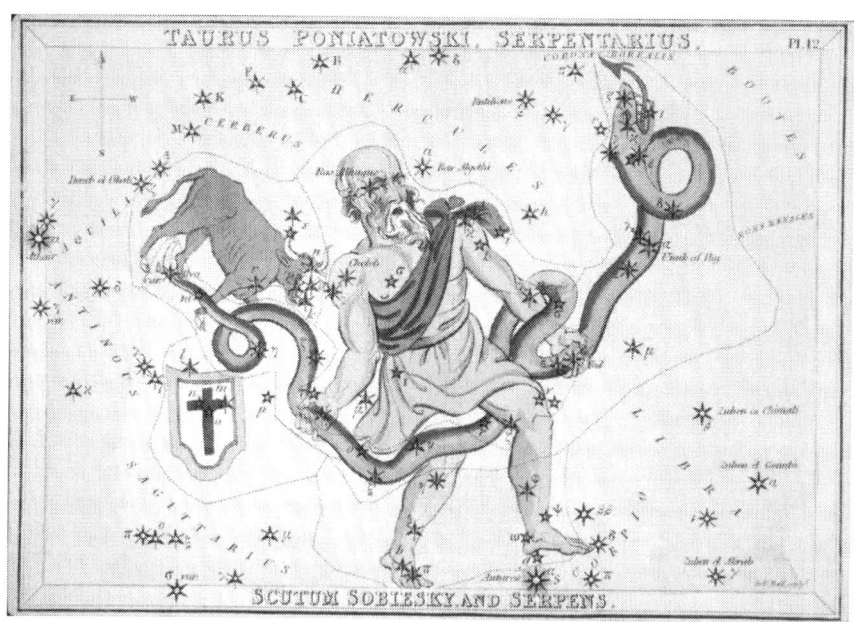

---

[88] Deuteronomy 8:15

Ophiuchus is a man standing with one foot on the scorpion (Scorpio), holding up a serpent (Serpens). Ophiuchus is Moses holding the bronze serpent God commanded him to make and place on a pole.[89] Those who looked at Moses' bronze serpent were healed of their snake bites.

That Ophiuchus and Serpens is Moses and the bronze serpent is shown by the same constellation being associated with the serpent on the pole emblem which has been used since ancient times to represent healing and medicine.[90] It can be seen on ambulances and medical buildings. This symbol originated as a corruption of the biblical story of Moses' brass serpent on a pole.

We saw in Virgo the promise of the "Branch," the coming Messiah. In Libra, we saw that the Law itself contains symbolic imagery of the ultimate sacrifice for sins in the Passover and other animal sacrifices. In Scorpio, with the Israelites suffering the sting of God's rejection in the wilderness, again there is hope proclaimed by the serpent on the pole. Jesus Himself interpreted the meaning, applying the symbolism to His upcoming crucifixion as a remedy for our bite of the serpent – sin. *"As Moses lifted up the serpent in the*

---

[89] Numbers 21:8-9
[90] Ridpath, Ian, Star Tales, Ophiuchus,
http://www.ianridpath.com/startales/ophiuchus.htm

wilderness, even so must the Son of Man be lifted up, that whoever believes in Him should not perish but have eternal life."[91]

These three constellations, the scorpion, the scales at the scorpion's claws, and the snake holder with his right foot on the scorpion, paint a complete picture. They point to the Law (Libra), its penalty (Scorpio), and the promise of redemption from the Law (Ophiuchus). Jesus was the One to fulfill that promise when, just as Moses lifted up the serpent on a pole, Jesus was hung on a cross. And all who look to Him find salvation from the venom of the serpents and scorpions.

---

[91] John 3:14-15

Chapter 6
Sagittarius
The Promised Land Realized

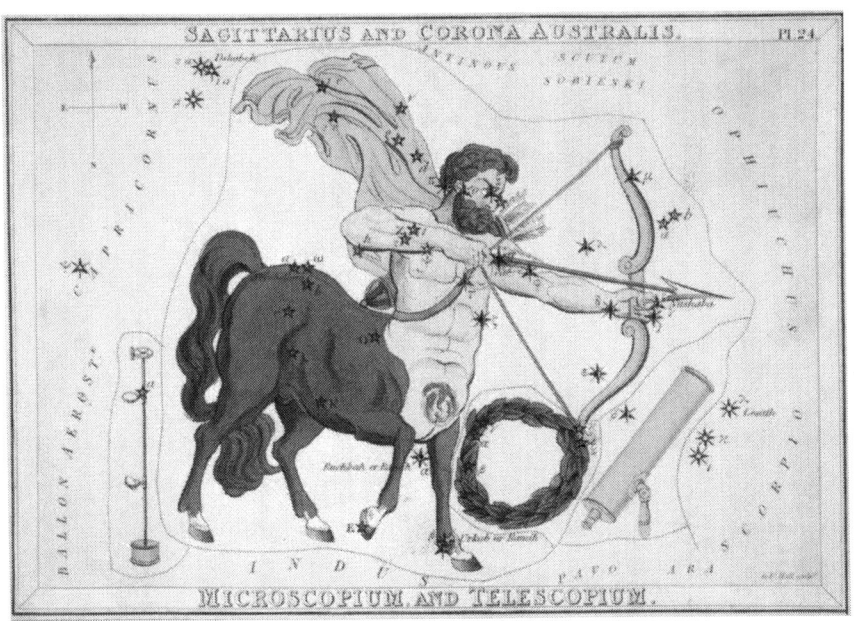

Joshua 1:1-6
1 After the death of Moses the servant of the LORD, it came to pass that the LORD spoke to Joshua the son of Nun, Moses' assistant, saying:
2 "Moses My servant is dead. Now therefore, arise, go over this Jordan, you and all this people, to the land which I am giving to them—the children of Israel.
3 Every place that the sole of your foot will tread upon I have given you, as I said to Moses. 4 From the wilderness and this

MYSTERY of the MAZZAROTH

Lebanon as far as the great river, the River Euphrates, all the land of the Hittites, and to the Great Sea toward the going down of the sun, shall be your territory. 5 No man shall be able to stand before you all the days of your life; as I was with Moses, so I will be with you. I will not leave you nor forsake you.
6 Be strong and of good courage, for to this people you shall divide as an inheritance the land which I swore to their fathers to give them.

Sagittarius is a representation of an archer on horseback – a warrior. When Jacob blessed his sons on his death-bed, he prophesied regarding the tribe of Joseph: *"His bow remained in strength, And the arms of his hands were made strong by the hands of the Mighty God of Jacob. … The blessings of your father have excelled the blessings of my ancestors, Up to the utmost bound of the everlasting hills. They shall be on the head of Joseph, And on the crown of the head of him who was separate from his brothers."*[92] Jacob's blessing references Joseph's tribe as being archers whose arms are strengthened by God Himself to draw the bow. The blessings of Jacob are said to be a crown on his head.

Sagittarius is an archer riding a horse. Joshua, Moses' successor, was of the tribe of Joseph.[93] Jacob's prophecy was fulfilled in Joshua's military campaigns to drive out the inhabitants of the Promised Land in the strength of the Lord, and divide the land as an inheritance to the twelve tribes of Israel.

---
[92] Genesis 49:24, 26
[93] Genesis 41:51-52; Numbers 13:8, 16

MYSTERY of the MAZZAROTH

Joshua's military success was not of his own strength or cunning. Without the God of Abraham going with him into battle, there was no hope of victory. The Israelites were outnumbered in almost every battle, and usually at a huge strategic disadvantage. Yet again and again miracles occurred on the battlefield. The first such miracle was at Jericho. Through simple obedience to what seemed like an absurd battle strategy, God knocked down the walls of Jericho and handed Joshua his first victory in the Promised Land.

Unfortunately, that success was short lived. God had given the Israelites specific orders concerning the booty. One man's disobedience to that order resulted in God's abandoning the Israelites in their next battle for Ai. They were defeated, and ran in terror before their enemies.

> *Joshua 7:6-12*
> *6 Then Joshua tore his clothes, and fell to the earth on his face before the ark of the LORD until evening, he and the elders of Israel; and they put dust on their heads.*
> *7 And Joshua said, "Alas, Lord GOD, why have You brought this people over the Jordan at all — to deliver us into the hand of the Amorites, to destroy us? Oh, that we had been content, and dwelt on the other side of the Jordan!*
> *8 O Lord, what shall I say when Israel turns its back before its enemies?*
> *9 For the Canaanites and all the inhabitants of the land will hear it, and surround us, and cut off our name from the earth. Then what will You do for Your great name?"*
> *10 So the LORD said to Joshua: "Get up! Why do you lie thus on your face?*

> *11 Israel has sinned, and they have also transgressed My covenant which I commanded them. For they have even taken some of the accursed things, and have both stolen and deceived; and they have also put it among their own stuff.*
>
> *12 Therefore the children of Israel could not stand before their enemies, but turned their backs before their enemies, because they have become doomed to destruction. Neither will I be with you anymore, unless you destroy the accursed from among you."*

This defeat taught Israel a very difficult lesson regarding their relationship with this God who brought them out of Egypt. They were utterly dependent upon God's power and presence in battle to deliver on His promises of the land inheritance. One cannot take God's presence for granted. As Scorpio taught them, God withdraws from sin and disobedience with very painful results. He takes His power and promises with Him. During these battles, the Israelites were being supported by God's mighty hand alone. There was no safety net of their own making. They were in a foreign land behind enemy lines. They were greatly outnumbered and had no continuous stream of supplies. Without God's continuous protection, provision, and power unleashed in battle, they would be quickly dispatched. They soon learned that careless disobedience is deadly in such a precarious situation. The sweet taste of victory that comes with an utter dependence on an all-powerful God can very quickly turn to bitterness when He is offended.

God could easily have defeated the wicked inhabitants of Canaan without Joshua's help. After all, He didn't need

Joshua or the Israelites to bring about the flood in Noah's day, or to wipe out Sodom and Gomorrah. Yet, God entrusted His arrows of justice to Joshua and the nation of Israel. He had Israel play the part of God's executioner. In some cases, God commanded Joshua to spare absolutely no one, not even women and children. Why? For the same reason God spared only Noah and his family from the flood, and Lot and his daughters from the destruction of Sodom. There are times when a cancer must be cut out, or when a gangrenous limb must be amputated for the greater good. God wanted Joshua and the Israelites to see, up close and personal, what happens to those who have completely rejected God and given themselves over to total depravity,[94] like witchcraft, burning their children alive as sacrifices to demon-gods, or open perversions of God's well-designed order.

> *Deut. 18:9-14*
> *9 "When you come into the land which the LORD your God is giving you, you shall not learn to follow the abominations of those nations. 10 There shall not be found among you anyone who makes his son or his daughter pass through the fire, or one who practices witchcraft, or a soothsayer, or one who interprets omens, or a sorcerer, 11 or one who conjures spells, or a medium, or a spiritist, or one who calls up the dead. 12 For all who do these things are an abomination to the LORD, and because of these abominations the LORD your God drives them out from before you. 13 You shall be blameless before the LORD your God. 14 For these nations which you will dispossess listened to soothsayers and*

---

[94] Rom. 1:18-32

diviners; but as for you, the LORD your God has not appointed such for you."

There is nothing to be spared from such a population that would infect God's people with the same fatal disease. God pronounced these whole societies as "worthy of death" and sent Joshua to carry out the just sentence. Joshua led the Israelites in many successful battles where they were greatly outnumbered. No one could question that Joshua's military victories were due to Israel's God – Jehovah.

> *Josh. 10:7-11*
> *7 So Joshua ascended from Gilgal, he and all the people of war with him, and all the mighty men of valor. 8 And the LORD said to Joshua, "Do not fear them, for I have delivered them into your hand; not a man of them shall stand before you." 9 Joshua therefore came upon them suddenly, having marched all night from Gilgal. 10 So the LORD routed them before Israel, killed them with a great slaughter at Gibeon, chased them along the road that goes to Beth Horon, and struck them down as far as Azekah and Makkedah. 11 And it happened, as they fled before Israel and were on the descent of Beth Horon, that the LORD cast down large hailstones from heaven on them as far as Azekah, and they died. There were more who died from the hailstones than the children of Israel killed with the sword.*

Eventually, Joshua divided the land among the twelve tribes as their inheritance. Farming and animal husbandry began to occupy their time instead of war. The land indeed was "flowing with milk and honey." God prospered Israel greatly in their new home, with abundant crops and herds. God's presence among them was now realized through prosperity instead of victory in battle.

But after Joshua's death, old habits returned. Just as Moses had warned, prosperity had its own pitfalls.

> *Deut. 8:11-20*
> *11 "Beware that you do not forget the LORD your God by not keeping His commandments, His judgments, and His statutes which I command you today,*
> *12 lest — when you have eaten and are full, and have built beautiful houses and dwell in them; 13 and when your herds and your flocks multiply, and your silver and your gold are multiplied, and all that you have is multiplied; 14 when your heart is lifted up, and you forget the LORD your God who brought you out of the land of Egypt, from the house of bondage; 15 who led you through that great and terrible wilderness, in which were fiery serpents and scorpions and thirsty land where there was no water; who brought water for you out of the flinty rock; 16 who fed you in the wilderness with manna, which your fathers did not know, that He might humble you and that He might test you, to do you good in the end — 17 then you say in your heart, 'My power and the might of my hand have gained me this wealth.'*
> *18 "And you shall remember the LORD your God, for it is He who gives you power to get wealth, that He may establish His covenant which He swore to your fathers, as it is this day.*

> *19 Then it shall be, if you by any means forget the LORD your God, and follow other gods, and serve them and worship them, I testify against you this day that you shall surely perish. 20 As the nations which the LORD destroys before you, so you shall perish, because you would not be obedient to the voice of the LORD your God."*

Sure enough, prosperity led to complacency. Once again, they forgot the source of their prosperity, and the truth that *"every good and perfect gift is from above, and comes down from the Father of lights."*[95] Instead of pursuing a relationship with the God who continually demonstrated His love through abundant material blessings, they became proud and arrogant, supposing that they were getting what they deserved or had obtained by their own skill and power.

God used Israel to destroy these nations so that they would understand just how appalling the pagan practices were to a holy God. Yet, instead they gradually began to adopt many of the pagan customs, all of which were highly offensive to God and His just nature. More hard lessons lay ahead for the chosen nation before they could learn to appreciate the only thing of real value—the presence of God, before they would come to appreciate His just character, and understand their own shortcomings.

---

[95] James 1:17

Chapter 7
Capricorn
The Davidic Covenant

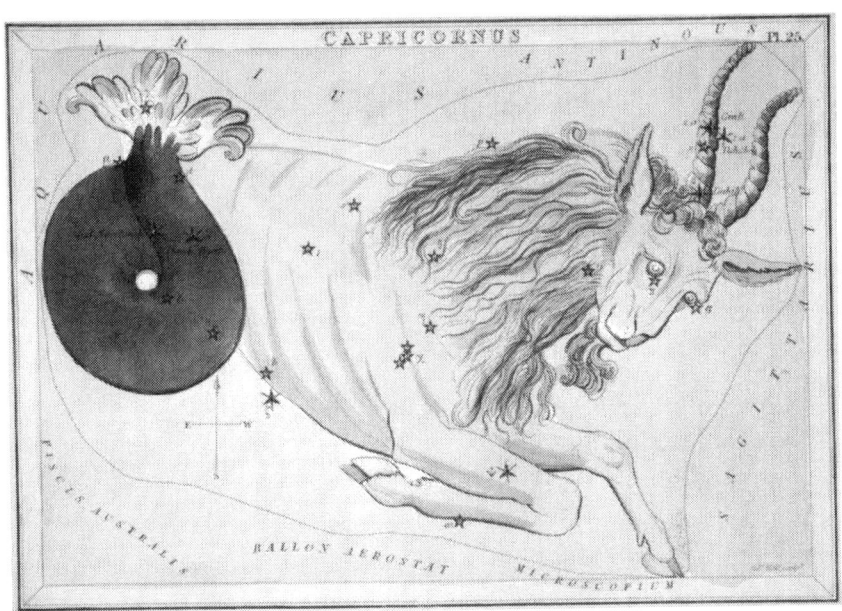

1 Samuel 23:29 – 24:21
*29 Then David went up from there and dwelt in strongholds at **<u>En Gedi</u>**.*
*24:1 Now it happened, when Saul had returned from following the Philistines, that it was told him, saying, "Take note! David is in the Wilderness of En Gedi." 2 Then Saul took three thousand chosen men from all Israel, and went to seek David and his men on **<u>the Rocks of the Wild Goats</u>**.*

MYSTERY of the MAZZAROTH

There were brief periods in Israel's history when they followed the God of Abraham, Isaac, and Jacob. It was when they had strong leaders who had a heart for God, leaders like Moses and Joshua. After many setbacks and trials in the Promised Land due to their wavering commitment, God once again raised up a strong leader. David was "a man after God's own heart." His heart is revealed in many of his Psalms. Even as a teen, his great faith was displayed in his defeat of Goliath, trusting in the God of Israel. God saw in David someone He could mold into a great leader.

After David's defeat of the Philistine giant, God began using him to complete the work Joshua had left undone, ridding the Promised Land of the remaining pagans and their detestable practices. Like Joshua before him, the power of God was evident with David as he led his band of loyal warriors in battle after battle.

Saul had proven himself unfit for the throne of Israel, repeatedly refusing to obey the Lord and acting presumptuously. So, God sent Samuel the prophet secretly to the home of Jesse in Bethlehem to anoint David his son as Israel's future king. When this became known, Saul made it his mission in life to hunt down David and kill him.

David was forced to spend years on the run, hiding from Saul. There is no sharper contrast exposed between Saul and David than when David refused to harm Saul at En Gedi and seize the throne, even though he had a clear opportunity to do so. David would not take things into his own hands, leaving it to God to bring about His promise to install him as king. David reflected the heart of Jesus' later command to *"love your enemies, bless those who curse you, do good to those who hate you, and pray for those who spitefully use you and persecute you, that you may be sons of your Father in heaven."*[96]

Capricorn represents the covenant God made with David, the shepherd-king. God promised to raise up from David's seed a King who would reign upon David's throne over the house of Israel forever.[97]

While David was awaiting God's promise to install him on the throne of Israel, he and his loyal band established a hideout from Saul and his army in a desert oasis along the western side of the Dead Sea, called En Gedi, which means "the goats." The synagogue zodiacs label Capricorn as "En Gedi." It is a one square mile haven, bordered on the north, west, and south by many miles of desert and barren rocky mountains. The Dead Sea stretches out to the east. This Sea is so salty that no fish can survive.

Yet within this harsh and forbidding wasteland, En Gedi is teeming with animal and plant life, being fed by fresh water springs pouring out of crevices in the rocks, producing beautiful waterfalls and pools. It gets its name from the wild mountain goats that inhabit the area. En Gedi is a fitting setting for a man like David—a jewel in the midst of a wasteland.

---

[96] Matt 5:44-45
[97] Psalm 132:10-18; Isaiah 9:6-7; Luke 1:30-33; Acts 2:30

En Gedi's connection to David is not just limited to David's hideout. It is also famous for Ezekiel's prophecy of Christ's coming Kingdom. David's promised descendant will one day take His rightful place on David's throne to reign forever from Jerusalem over the restored earth. The barren desert will "blossom like a rose."[98] En Gedi will be transformed into a fishing paradise. The Dead Sea will be healed, and yield an abundance of fish for the fishermen of En Gedi.

> *Ezekiel 47:7-10*
> *8 Then he said to me: "This water flows toward the eastern region, goes down into the valley, and enters the sea. When it reaches the sea, its waters are healed. 9 And it shall be that every living thing that moves, wherever the rivers go, will live. There will be a very great multitude of fish, because these waters go there; for they will be healed, and everything will live wherever the river goes. 10 It shall be that fishermen will stand by it from En Gedi to En Eglaim; they will be places for spreading their nets. Their fish will be of the same kinds as the fish of the Great Sea, exceedingly many.*

Capricorn the goat-fish represents David's royal story from beginning (the upper body of a mountain goat) to end (the tail of a fish). It begins with his hiding out among the mountain goats of En Gedi in this tiny oasis, being hunted by Saul who continued to reign for several years. It ends with the fulfillment of God's promise — the Davidic King of David's royal dynasty reigning forever, with David's old hideout transformed into Israel's premier fishing paradise. The whole

---

[98] Isaiah 35:1

land of Israel will become one big oasis. The springs of En Gedi that today empty a small amount of fresh water into the Dead Sea are symbolic of the mighty river of healing water that will flow from David's Throne in the Jerusalem Temple, healing everything it touches, including the entire Dead Sea.[99]

Capricorn in Greek Mythology

The Greeks identified the god Pan with Capricorn. Pan was the god of shepherds and flocks, and was known for his invention of musical instruments and skill in playing. The "panpipe" was also known as the "shepherd's pipe," and was said to be the invention of Pan. David was a shepherd and musician. He composed the fifth Psalm for the panpipe.[100]

Toward the end of his reign, in settling the dispute over who would succeed him to the throne, David commanded Nathan the prophet and Zadok the priest to lead Solomon in a public procession to proclaim him the rightful heir. *"And Zadok the priest took an horn of oil out of the tabernacle, and anointed Solomon. And they blew the trumpet; and all the people said, God save king Solomon. And all the people came up after him, and __the people piped with pipes__, and rejoiced with great joy, so that the earth rent with the sound of them."*[101] The celebration with panpipes was in honor of David and his choice of successor.

Pan was also said to love dancing. However, the goddesses (Nymphs) considered his dancing to be crude and lacking in modesty. *"Pan, the Nymphai say, dances badly and goes beyond*

---

[99] Ezekiel 47:1-12; Zechariah 14:8-11; Revelation 22:1-3
[100] Psalm 5:1 heading
[101] 1 Kings 1:39-40 KJV

bounds in his leaping, leaping up and jumping aloft after the manner of sportive goats; and they say that they would teach him a different kind of dancing, or a more delightful character."[102] This aspect of the Pan myth is strikingly similar to David's procession, bringing the Ark of the Covenant to Jerusalem after defeating the Jebusites.

> *2 Sam 6:14-16, 20-22*
> *14 Then David danced before the LORD with all his might; and David was wearing a linen ephod. 15 So David and all the house of Israel brought up the ark of the LORD with shouting and with the sound of the trumpet.*
> *16 Now as the ark of the LORD came into the City of David, Michal, Saul's daughter, looked through a window and saw King David leaping and whirling before the LORD; and she despised him in her heart. ...*
> *20 ... And Michal the daughter of Saul came out to meet David, and said, "How glorious was the king of Israel today, uncovering himself today in the eyes of the maids of his servants, as one of the base fellows shamelessly uncovers himself!"*
> *21 So David said to Michal, "It was before the LORD, who chose me instead of your father and all his house, to appoint me ruler over the people of the LORD, over Israel. Therefore I will play music before the LORD.*
> *22 And I will be even more undignified than this, and will be humble in my own sight. But as for the maidservants of whom you have spoken, by them I will be held in honor."*

---

[102] http://www.theoi.com/Georgikos/Pan.html

Another interesting feature of the Greek Pan mythology is the existence of a whole group of "Pans" in addition to the original Pan. This legend may have been a corruption of an original prophecy of the Davidic dynasty, the series of kings from David's seed who reigned upon David's throne over Judah.

The Davidic Covenant and the Branch in Virgo's Hand
The coming Messiah promised in the Davidic Covenant is a further development of the Branch motif in Virgo's right hand. What is promised only in symbol in the first constellation is now more clearly revealed in Capricorn. The Branch is one of Abraham's offspring. He comes through David's royal line as the rightful heir to the Throne of David.

> *Isaiah 4:2-4*
> *2 In that day **the Branch** of the LORD shall be beautiful and glorious; And the fruit of the earth shall be excellent and appealing For those of Israel who have escaped.*
> *3 And it shall come to pass that he who is left in Zion and remains in Jerusalem will be called holy — everyone who is recorded among the living in Jerusalem.*
> *4 When the Lord has washed away the filth of the daughters of Zion, and purged the blood of Jerusalem from her midst, by the spirit of judgment and by the spirit of burning.*

> *Isaiah 11:1-6*
> *1 There shall come forth **a Rod** from the stem of Jesse, And **a Branch** shall grow out of his roots. 2 The Spirit of the LORD shall rest upon Him, The Spirit of wisdom and*

understanding, The Spirit of counsel and might, The Spirit of knowledge and of the fear of the LORD.

3 His delight is in the fear of the LORD, And He shall not judge by the sight of His eyes, Nor decide by the hearing of His ears;

4 But with righteousness He shall judge the poor, And decide with equity for the meek of the earth; He shall strike the earth with the rod of His mouth, And with the breath of His lips He shall slay the wicked.

5 Righteousness shall be the belt of His loins, And faithfulness the belt of His waist.

6 "The wolf also shall dwell with the lamb, The leopard shall lie down with the young goat, The calf and the young lion and the fatling together; And a little child shall lead them."

Jeremiah 33:14-17

14 'Behold, the days are coming,' says the LORD, 'that I will perform that good thing which I have promised to the house of Israel and to the house of Judah:

15 'In those days and at that time I will cause to grow up to David **A Branch** of righteousness; He shall execute judgment and righteousness in the earth.

16 In those days Judah will be saved, And Jerusalem will dwell safely. And this is the name by which she will be called: THE LORD OUR RIGHTEOUSNESS.'

17 "For thus says the LORD: 'David shall never lack a man to sit on the throne of the house of Israel.'"

God's covenant with David was to be fulfilled with the birth of a child.

MYSTERY of the MAZZAROTH

Isaiah 9:6-7
6 For unto us a Child is born, Unto us a Son is given; And the government will be upon His shoulder. And His name will be called Wonderful Counselor, Mighty God, Everlasting Father, Prince of Peace.
7 Of the increase of His government and peace There will be no end, Upon the throne of David and over His kingdom, To order it and establish it with judgment and justice From that time forward, even forever. The zeal of the Lord of hosts will perform this.

Failure of the Davidic Dynasty

While David was indeed a man after God's own heart, his kingdom soon deteriorated as the generations passed and his sons forsook the God of their father. Solomon reigned well for many years after David's death, but eventually Solomon's many pagan wives turned his heart away from serving the God of Israel, just as God had warned him.[103] Solomon introduced Israel to many pagan gods, corrupting the monarchy and the whole nation. Upon his death, there was a power struggle for succession to the throne of David which tore the nation apart. The northern ten tribes (Israel) followed Jeroboam, and the southern two tribes (Judah) followed Solomon's son, Rehoboam.

Because Jeroboam sought to solidify his reign over the northern tribes, he immediately established an alternate place of worship in Samaria in order to discourage the people from going to Jerusalem to worship at Solomon's Temple.

---
[103] 1 Kings 11:1-13

MYSTERY of the MAZZAROTH

1 Kings 12:27-33
27 If these people go up to offer sacrifices in the house of the LORD at Jerusalem, then the heart of this people will turn back to their lord, Rehoboam king of Judah, and they will kill me and go back to Rehoboam king of Judah."
28 Therefore the king asked advice, made two calves of gold, and said to the people, "It is too much for you to go up to Jerusalem. Here are your gods, O Israel, which brought you up from the land of Egypt!"
29 And he set up one in Bethel, and the other he put in Dan.
30 Now this thing became a sin, for the people went to worship before the one as far as Dan.
31 He made shrines on the high places, and made priests from every class of people, who were not of the sons of Levi.
32 Jeroboam ordained a feast on the fifteenth day of the eighth month,[104] like the feast that was in Judah, and offered sacrifices on the altar. So he did at Bethel, sacrificing to the calves that he had made. And at Bethel he installed the priests of the high places which he had made.
33 So he made offerings on the altar which he had made at Bethel on the fifteenth day of the eighth month, in the month which he had devised in his own heart. And he ordained a feast for the children of Israel, and offered sacrifices on the altar and burned incense.

All of the succeeding kings of the northern kingdom were steeped in idolatry and worship of pagan idols. Eventually, God sent His judgment upon them, sending the king of Assyria to defeat them and carry them off as slaves to Assyria.

---

[104] The possible origin of Halloween, since it often occurs on this day.

The southern kingdom continued for many years with the Davidic dynasty intact. Some of the Davidic kings followed the Lord, but many did not. Finally, the Lord sent His prophets to pronounce doom on the southern kingdom as well, and an end to the Davidic dynasty. Because King Josiah feared the Lord and walked in the ways of David his father, God promised to delay judgment until after his death.

Israel's former lessons faded from view as new generations emerged, and fathers failed to instruct their children in Israel's history with the God of Abraham. Israel's instruction through God's direct intervention in their history was intended to gradually elevate their understanding of both God and man, and His purpose in human history. Everything was geared towards educating them and developing them into a people with whom God could have an enduring and lasting relationship of mutual love. Yet, this nation continuously turned aside and failed to learn that the only meaningful pursuit in heaven and earth is the pursuit of the Creator of heaven and earth.

Yet, God made a promise to David which He cannot break. The Messiah would indeed come and take the Throne of David, and rule forever.

> *Isaiah 9:6-7*
> *6 For unto us a Child is born, Unto us a Son is given; And the government will be upon His shoulder. And His name will be called Wonderful, Counselor, Mighty God, Everlasting Father, Prince of Peace.*

7 Of the increase of His government and peace There will be no end, Upon the throne of David and over His kingdom, To order it and establish it with judgment and justice From that time forward, even forever. The zeal of the Lord of hosts will perform this.

This Son of David was born a thousand years after God's covenant with David, and about eight hundred years from Isaiah's prophecy.

Chapter 8
Aquarius
The Babylonian Exile

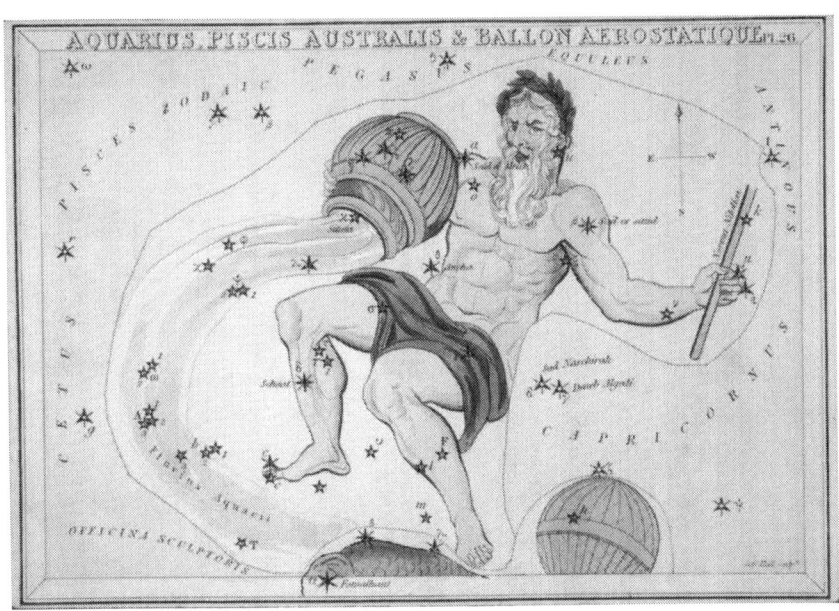

Jeremiah 1:13-16 NIV
13 The word of the LORD came to me again: "What do you see?" "<u>I see a boiling pot, tilting away from the north</u>," I answered.
14 The LORD said to me, "From the north <u>disaster will be poured out on all who live in the land</u>.
15 I am about to summon all the peoples of the northern kingdoms," declares the LORD. "Their kings will come and set up their thrones in the entrance of the gates of Jerusalem;

MYSTERY of the MAZZAROTH

they will come against all her surrounding walls and against all the towns of Judah.
16 I will pronounce my judgments on my people because of their wickedness in forsaking me, in burning incense to other gods and in worshiping what their hands have made.

Forty years before the destruction of Jerusalem, God called Jeremiah to be his final prophet sent to warn Judah of the coming invasion and destruction by Nebuchadnezzar. Jeremiah was first shown the coming judgment on Jerusalem through a vision of a large boiling cauldron with its mouth pointing away from the north.

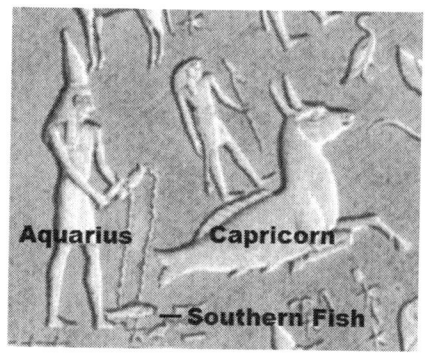

Aquarius is a representation of Nebuchadnezzar pouring out God's fury upon the southern kingdom of Judah – which is represented by the Southern Fish (Piscis Austrinus). Originally, the Southern Fish was part of Aquarius, as the Dendera zodiac shows.

Just before the complete destruction of Jerusalem, when Nebuchadnezzar began his siege of the city, God gave Ezekiel a similar vision of a boiling cauldron.

Ezekiel 24:1-14
1 Again, in the ninth year, in the tenth month, on the tenth day of the month, the word of the LORD came to me, saying,

2 "Son of man, write down the name of the day, this very day — the king of Babylon started his siege against Jerusalem this very day.
3 And utter a parable to the rebellious house, and say to them, 'Thus says the Lord GOD:
"Put on a pot, set it on, And also pour water into it.
4 Gather pieces of meat in it, Every good piece, The thigh and the shoulder. Fill it with choice cuts;
5 Take the choice of the flock. Also pile fuel bones under it, Make it boil well, And let the cuts simmer in it."
6 Therefore thus says the Lord GOD:
"Woe to the bloody city, To the pot whose scum is in it, And whose scum is not gone from it! Bring it out piece by piece, On which no lot has fallen.
7 For her blood is in her midst; She set it on top of a rock; She did not pour it on the ground, To cover it with dust.
8 That it may raise up fury and take vengeance, I have set her blood on top of a rock, That it may not be covered."
9 Therefore thus says the Lord GOD:
"Woe to the bloody city! I too will make the pyre great.
10 Heap on the wood, Kindle the fire; Cook the meat well, Mix in the spices, And let the cuts be burned up.
11 "Then set the pot empty on the coals, That it may become hot and its bronze may burn, That its filthiness may be melted in it, That its scum may be consumed.
12 She has grown weary with lies, And her great scum has not gone from her. Let her scum be in the fire!
13 In your filthiness is lewdness. Because I have cleansed you, and you were not cleansed, You will not be cleansed of your filthiness anymore, Till I have caused My fury to rest upon you.

> *14 I, the LORD, have spoken it; It shall come to pass, and I will do it; I will not hold back, Nor will I spare, Nor will I relent; According to your ways And according to your deeds They will judge you," Says the Lord GOD.*

In Ezekiel's vision, God prophesied the destruction of Jerusalem by Nebuchadnezzar and the Babylonian armies. Jerusalem was a giant boiling pot. The cuts of meat boiling in the pot were the people of Judah. God was going to turn up the heat of His fury using Nebuchadnezzar. Then, after the food was completely cooked, He was going to let the cauldron stay in the fire to completely burn up the scum.

In the Babylonian star catalogue, MUL.APIN, Aquarius is called "GU.LA" meaning "the Mighty One." This is precisely what God called Nebuchadnezzar in Ezekiel's prophecy about the Assyrians who were also crushed by Nebuchadnezzar and his hordes. *"Therefore thus says the Lord GOD: 'Because you have increased in height, and it set its top among the thick boughs, and its heart was lifted up in its height, therefore I will deliver it into the hand of **the mighty one** of the nations, and he shall surely deal with it; I have driven it out for its wickedness."*[105]

A repeating pattern is now becoming evident. Virgo illustrated God's covenant with Abraham with great promises for Abraham and his descendants. In Libra, the Law was given as a righteous standard requiring obedience and single-minded dedication to God. He brought His chosen nation out

---
[105] Ezekiel 31:10-11

of slavery with a mighty hand, through the wilderness, providing food, water, and His protection from their enemies. Yet, even with His presence going with them, and with many miraculous demonstrations provided along the way to the Promised Land, they rebelled against Him. The result was His severe judgment seen in Scorpio.

Still, for the sake of His covenant with Abraham (and for His own Name), the Lord again extended His powerful arm on Israel's behalf, defeating their enemies through Joshua and delivering the land He promised to the twelve tribes. With Capricorn came the Davidic covenant, a renewed promise of a future permanent inheritance of the Land and everlasting peace,[106] when David's promised Seed will reign upon his throne. But, once again, God's blessings and prosperity led to complacency and ingratitude. The kings of Israel and Judah turned away from God to worship the gods of the nations. They despised His promises and persecuted His prophets, leading the whole nation into rebellion.

The judgment seen in Scorpio, God's rejection of that generation because of their rejection of Him and His promises, is repeated in Aquarius, as God again turns His face from a rebellious nation for discipline. This time, rather than turning them over to scorpions and serpents, He turned them over to their enemies. After having delivered them from slavery in Egypt and handing them the Promised Land through many amazing miracles, He then sent them into captivity in Babylon, this time for seventy years of servitude.

---

[106] Psalm 37

As a final crushing blow, Nebuchadnezzar attacked Jerusalem, demolished Solomon's Temple, killed the high priest, carried off the gold and silver vessels of the house of God, and broke down Jerusalem's walls. She lay desolate and abandoned for seventy years, like a raped and plundered prostitute lying on the side of the road, nearly dead. The nation God called to be His bride had played the harlot once too many times.

> *Lamentations (of Jeremiah) 1:1-3*
>
> *1 How lonely sits the city That was full of people! How like a widow is she, Who was great among the nations! The princess among the provinces Has become a slave!*
>
> *2 She weeps bitterly in the night, Her tears are on her cheeks; Among all her lovers She has none to comfort her. All her friends have dealt treacherously with her; They have become her enemies.*
>
> *3 Judah has gone into captivity, Under affliction and hard servitude; She dwells among the nations, She finds no rest; All her persecutors overtake her in dire straits.*

Chapter 9
Pisces
The Return from Captivity

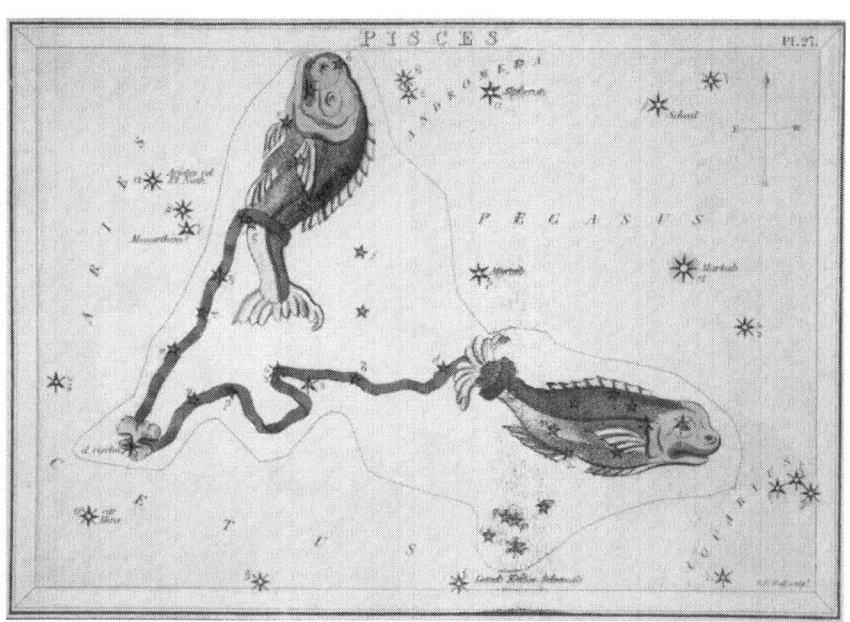

Jeremiah 16:14-16
14 "Therefore behold, the days are coming," says the LORD, "that it shall no more be said, 'The LORD lives who brought up the children of Israel from the land of Egypt,' 15 but, 'The LORD lives who brought up the children of Israel from the land of the north and from all the lands where He had driven them.' For I will bring them back into their land which I gave to their fathers. "Behold, I will send for many fishermen," says the LORD, "and they shall fish them."

MYSTERY of the MAZZAROTH

Hosea 11:4
4 I drew them with gentle cords, With bands of love, And I was to them as those who take the yoke from their neck. I stooped and fed them.

In the constellation Aquarius, the southern fish represented Judah undergoing God's wrath, and going into captivity in Babylon. In Pisces, the star where the two bands connect is called, "Al Rescha," Arabic for "the cords."

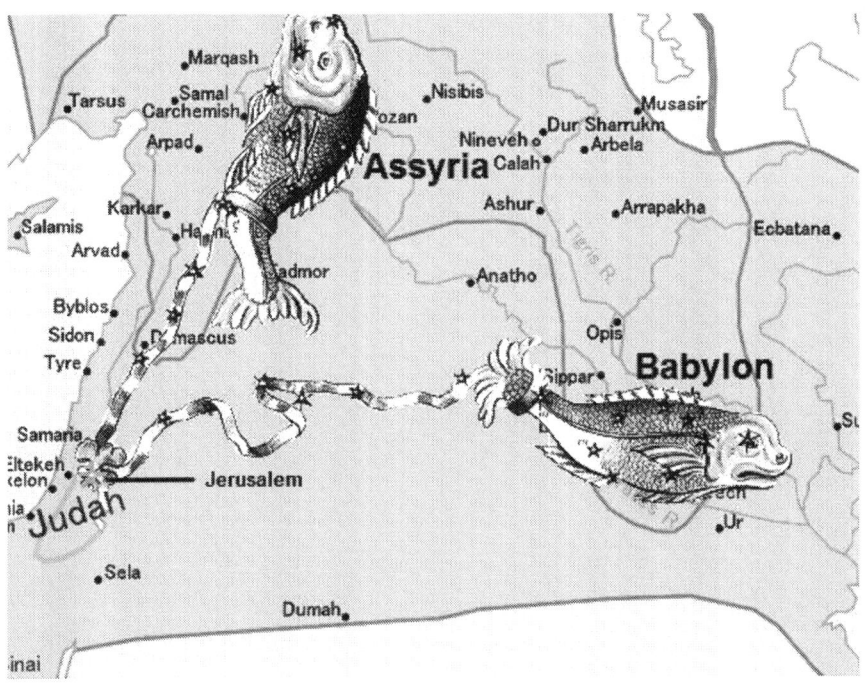

The constellation Pisces appears to be a map of the Middle East superimposed on the sky. The star where the cords join is Jerusalem. The fish to the right (east) is the southern kingdom of Judah as captive in Babylon, due east of Israel. The fish to the northeast is the northern kingdom of Israel as captive in

Assyria. The two fish being pulled by their tails represent Israel and Judah returning to the Promised Land by God's mercy and power, not by their own strength.

Many claim that the northern tribes are "lost tribes," and that they have never returned to the land of Israel. While it is true that many of those in the Assyrian captivity were assimilated and never returned, many did return. When the Babylonians defeated the Assyrians prior to the captivity of Judah, the Babylonians gained control over the Assyrian territory, Samaria, and the northern captives in Assyria. When the Persians overthrew the Babylonians, they inherited the captives of Israel and Judah from both Assyria and Babylon. When Cyrus the Persian authorized the return of the captives to Israel to rebuild Jerusalem and the temple, his decree included all Israelites regardless of tribe. Scripture provides ample evidence that substantial segments of all twelve tribes returned from the captivity.

> *Ezra 1:1-4*
> *1 Now in the first year of Cyrus king of Persia, that **the word of the LORD by the mouth of Jeremiah might be fulfilled**, the LORD stirred up the spirit of Cyrus king of Persia, so that he made a proclamation throughout all his kingdom, and also put it in writing, saying,*
> *2 Thus says Cyrus king of Persia: All the kingdoms of the earth the LORD God of heaven has given me. And He has commanded me to build Him a house at Jerusalem which is in Judah. 3 **Who is among you of all His people**? May his God be with him, and let him go up to Jerusalem which is in Judah, and build the house of the LORD God of Israel (He is*

*God), which is in Jerusalem. 4 **<u>And whoever is left in any place where he dwells</u>**, let the men of his place help him with silver and gold, with goods and livestock, besides the freewill offerings for the house of God which is in Jerusalem.*

Notice that Cyrus' decree was the direct fulfillment of Jeremiah's prophecy. That prophecy concerned the return of both Israel and Judah, setting the stage for the New Covenant that God would make with the house of Israel and the house of Judah.

> *Jer 31:27-34*
> *27 "Behold, the days are coming, says the LORD, that I will sow **<u>the house of Israel and the house of Judah</u>** with the seed of man and the seed of beast. 28 And it shall come to pass, that as I have watched over them to pluck up, to break down, to throw down, to destroy, and to afflict, so I will watch over them to build and to plant, says the LORD. 29 In those days they shall say no more: 'The fathers have eaten sour grapes, And the children's teeth are set on edge.' 30 But every one shall die for his own iniquity; every man who eats the sour grapes, his teeth shall be set on edge.*
> *31 "Behold, the days are coming, says the LORD, when I will make a new covenant with the house of Israel and with the house of Judah— 32 not according to the covenant that I made with their fathers in the day that I took them by the hand to lead them out of the land of Egypt, My covenant which they broke, though I was a husband to them, says the LORD. 33 But this is the covenant that I will make with the house of Israel after those days, says the LORD: I will put My law in their minds, and write it on their hearts; and I*

will be their God, and they shall be My people. 34 No more shall every man teach his neighbor, and every man his brother, saying, 'Know the LORD,' for they all shall know Me, from the least of them to the greatest of them, says the LORD. For I will forgive their iniquity, and their sin I will remember no more."

The New Covenant was made with both the house of Israel and the house of Judah. The New Testament states plainly that the New Covenant was inaugurated by Jesus Christ.[107] This requires participants from both Israel and Judah at the time of Jesus Christ. Jesus sent his disciples ahead of Him to preach to "the lost sheep of the house of Israel."[108] In Paul's defense before Agrippa, he stated that all twelve tribes were currently serving God in Jerusalem in the hope of the resurrection.[109] Ezra informs us that when the rebuilt temple was dedicated shortly after the return under Cyrus the Great, all twelve tribes were represented in the resumption of Temple worship.

Ezra 6:15-18
15 Now the temple was finished on the third day of the month of Adar, which was in the sixth year of the reign of King Darius. 16 Then the children of Israel, the priests and the Levites and the rest of the descendants of the captivity, celebrated the dedication of this house of God with joy. 17 And they offered sacrifices at the dedication of this house of God, one hundred bulls, two hundred rams, four hundred

---

[107] Matthew 26:28; Hebrews 8:7-13
[108] Matthew 10:6
[109] Acts 26:7

*lambs, and **as a sin offering for all Israel twelve male goats, according to the number of the tribes of Israel**. 18 They assigned the priests to their divisions and the Levites to their divisions, over the service of God in Jerusalem, as it is written in the Book of Moses.*

The return from captivity was prophesied by Isaiah two hundred years before it occurred. This is one of the most astounding prophecies in Scripture. God sent a message by Isaiah to Cyrus king of Persia, long before he was born. The message declared that God was going to prosper him and give him success in his exploits and rise to power. God told Cyrus that he was going to decree the return from captivity of His people to rebuild Solomon's Temple.

Isaiah 44:24 – 45:4
24 Thus says the LORD, your Redeemer, And He who formed you from the womb: "I am the LORD, who makes all things, Who stretches out the heavens all alone, Who spreads abroad the earth by Myself; 25 Who frustrates the signs of the babblers, And drives diviners mad; Who turns wise men backward, And makes their knowledge foolishness;
26 Who confirms the word of His servant, And performs the counsel of His messengers; Who says to Jerusalem, 'You shall be inhabited,' To the cities of Judah, 'You shall be built,' And I will raise up her waste places; 27 Who says to the deep, 'Be dry! And I will dry up your rivers'; 28 Who says of Cyrus, 'He is My shepherd, And he shall perform all My pleasure, Saying to Jerusalem, "You shall be built," And to the temple, "Your foundation shall be laid."'

> 45:1 *"Thus says the LORD to His anointed, To Cyrus, whose right hand I have held — To subdue nations before him And loose the armor of kings, To open before him the double doors, So that the gates will not be shut: 2 'I will go before you And make the crooked places straight; I will break in pieces the gates of bronze And cut the bars of iron. 3 I will give you the treasures of darkness And hidden riches of secret places, That you may know that I, the LORD, Who call you by your name, Am the God of Israel. 4 For Jacob My servant's sake, And Israel My elect, I have even called you by your name; I have named you, though you have not known Me.*

However, notice God's remarks in chapter 44, verses 24-25 concerning the heavens. God identified Himself to Cyrus as *"the LORD, who makes all things, Who stretches out the heavens all alone, Who spreads abroad the earth by Myself; Who frustrates the signs of the babblers, And drives diviners mad; Who turns wise men backward, And makes their knowledge foolishness."* The association between stretching out the heavens and driving the astrologers mad makes one wonder if He had the sign of Pisces in mind! The One who spread out the constellations, including Aquarius and Pisces, raised up Nebuchadnezzar to punish Judah, and then raised up Cyrus to decree the return from captivity. In doing so, God turned the tables on the astrologers who claimed the ability to discern the constellations. It seems that God was telling Cyrus not to listen to his astrologers who pretend to understand the meaning of the zodiac, but instead listen to the One who designed it! As a token of His divinity, God gave Cyrus a sign, naming him and what he would do two centuries in advance.

Josephus explained what happened when Cyrus was shown this prophecy of Isaiah, written more than 200 years earlier.

> *"This was known to Cyrus by his reading the book which Isaiah left behind him of his prophecies; for this prophet said that God had spoken thus to him in a secret vision: "My will is, that Cyrus, whom I have appointed to be king over many and great nations, send back my people to their own land, and build my temple." This was foretold by Isaiah one hundred and forty years before the temple was demolished. Accordingly, when Cyrus read this, and admired the Divine power, an earnest desire and ambition seized upon him to fulfill what was so written; so he called for the most eminent Jews that were in Babylon, and said to them, that he gave them leave to go back to their own country, and to rebuild their city Jerusalem, and the temple of God, for that he would be their assistant, and that he would write to the rulers and governors that were in the neighborhood of their country of Judea, that they should contribute to them gold and silver for the building of the temple, and besides that, beasts for their sacrifices."*[110]

No wonder Cyrus was impressed! In his decree, Cyrus acknowledged the God of Israel and His providence in raising him to power for His own purposes. *"All the kingdoms of the earth the LORD God of heaven has given me. And He has*

---

[110] Josephus, Antiquities of the Jews, Book I, ch. 1:2

commanded me to build Him a house at Jerusalem which is in Judah."[111] He was known as "Cyrus the Great" because the God of Abraham made him great.

We began this chapter with Jeremiah's prophecy of the return from captivity from *"the land of the north and from all the lands where He had driven them."* This refers to both Israel and Judah. That God used the fishing metaphor for the return is particularly striking, since this is what Pisces depicts. *"Behold, I will send for many fishermen," says the LORD, "and they shall fish them."*

Like Sagittarius, Pisces shows the faithfulness of God despite the unfaithfulness of His people. Pisces brings us to the end of the Old Testament, setting the stage for the coming of the New Covenant prophesied by Jeremiah and the One who would inaugurate it – Aries, the Lamb of God.

The Name of the Branch Revealed

During the return, while the Temple was under construction, God revealed through Zechariah the prophet the name of the Messiah, the "Branch" in Virgo's hand from the line of David.

The first high priest who helped reconstruct the Temple was named Yeshua, according to the Hebrew text. In the Septuagint He is called Iesous. In English, it is Jesus. In the sixth chapter of Zechariah, God gave the prophet the following command: *"Thou shalt take silver and gold, and make crowns, and thou shalt put them upon the head of Jesus the son of*

---

[111] Ezra 1:2

Josedec the high priest."[112] Then, Zechariah was commanded to proclaim the following words to the gathered assembly: *"Look! The man, the Branch, the name is in him!"*[113] That is, the name of the "Branch" (the Messiah) was in Jesus the high priest, who was wearing the crowns. He was then instructed to place these crowns in the Temple as a memorial of those who had donated the gold and silver for Messiah's crowns.

The Branch is the Messiah. Zechariah identified His name as Yeshua in Hebrew, Iesous in Greek. This is why Gabriel instructed Mary to name the baby, Iesous (Jesus).[114] These very crowns, fashioned by the prophet Zechariah, will be worn by Jesus when He reigns in Jerusalem upon the Throne of David.

---

[112] Zechariah 6:11 LXX
[113] Our translation of Zechariah 6:12 from the LXX. The Greek has the pronoun "him" in the dative case, not the genitive case. This implies the preposition "in" should be supplied with the pronoun "him" ("is in him") rather than turning the pronoun into a possessive ("whose name is") as most translations render it.
[114] Luke 1:26-33

Chapter 10
Aries
The Lamb of the New Covenant

John 1:29-36

29 The next day John saw Jesus coming toward him, and said, "Behold! The Lamb of God who takes away the sin of the world! 30 This is He of whom I said, 'After me comes a Man who is preferred before me, for He was before me.' 31 I did not know Him; but that He should be revealed to Israel, therefore I came baptizing with water."

32 And John bore witness, saying, "I saw the Spirit descending from heaven like a dove, and He remained upon

Him. 33 I did not know Him, but He who sent me to baptize with water said to me, 'Upon whom you see the Spirit descending, and remaining on Him, this is He who baptizes with the Holy Spirit.' 34 And I have seen and testified that this is the Son of God."

35 Again, the next day, John stood with two of his disciples. 36 And looking at Jesus as He walked, he said, "Behold the Lamb of God!"

The story of Abraham's test of faith—God's asking him to sacrifice his only son Isaac—is loaded with prophetic imagery. Abraham's promised heir was about to be slaughtered. In the nick of time God provided a ram, caught by its horns in a thicket, as a substitute. Abraham's answer to his son's question, *"where is the lamb for a burnt offering,"* was clearly prophetic. *"God will provide Himself a lamb."*[115] Indeed, God did just that for Isaac. He also provided Himself a Lamb for the rest of mankind, and this offering did what the Law could not do: it made the descendants of Abraham righteous before God by means of a once-for-all substitutionary sacrifice. The ram sacrificed in Isaac's place prefigures the death of the Son of God.

Greek mythology surrounding Aries bears too many similarities to the story of Abraham to be coincidence.

> *"King Athamas and his wife Nephele had an unhappy marriage, so Athamas turned instead to Ino, daughter of King Cadmus from neighbouring Thebes. Ino resented her*

---

[115] Genesis 22:8

step-children, Phrixus and Helle, and she arranged a plot to have them killed. She began by parching the wheat so that the crops would fail. When Athamas appealed for help to the Delphic Oracle, Ino bribed messengers to bring back a false reply that Phrixus must be sacrificed to save the harvest. Reluctantly, Athamas, took his son to the top of Mount Laphystium, overlooking his palace at Orchomenus. He was about to sacrifice Phrixus to Zeus when Nephele intervened to save her son, sending down from the sky a winged ram with a golden fleece. ... Phrixus sacrificed the ram in gratitude to Zeus."[116]

King Athamas in the Greek myth is Abraham. His wife Nephele is Sarah. Ino is Hagar. She and her son Ishmael resented Isaac, the heir, represented in this myth as Phrixus. Athamas was about to sacrifice his son Phrixus to Zeus. Abraham was about to sacrifice his son Isaac to God. Just in the nick of time a ram was sent, who became the substitute for Phrixus. When Abraham was just about to plunge the knife into Isaac, God stopped him and provided the ram instead.

The story of Abraham predates the Greek myth by a millennium. The myth was almost certainly a corruption and embellishment of an oral historical account of Abraham. But the critical point is that the Greeks associated the constellation Aries with the substitute sacrificial ram in this Greek myth. In the Bible, the ram who died in Isaac's place prefigured Jesus Christ, the Lamb of God.

---

[116] Ridpath, Ian, Star Tales, Aries. http://www.ianridpath.com/startales/aries.htm

> *"Then Abraham lifted his eyes and looked, and there behind him was a ram caught in a thicket by its horns. So Abraham went and took the ram, and offered it up for a burnt offering instead of his son. And Abraham called the name of the place, The-LORD-Will-Provide; as it is said to this day, 'In the Mount of the LORD it shall be provided'."*[117]

The last sentence indicates that an oral tradition developed from this event, and this saying was still current about 400 years later when Moses penned the Torah. The saying still current in Moses' day was, *"In the Mount of the Lord it shall be provided."* The pronoun, "it," refers to a sacrificial lamb. The future tense verb (shall be provided) indicates this was prophecy. The saying that sprang from this episode was a prophecy of Jesus Christ, the Lamb whom God would one day provide. We have in this saying a direct link between the ram that was a substitute for Isaac and the "Lamb of God" identified by John the Baptist.

According to the Greek myth, *"Phrixos sacrificed the golden-fleeced ram to Zeus, but gave its fleece to Aeetes, who nailed it to an oak tree in a grove of Ares."*[118] The flesh of Jesus Christ, the Lamb of God, was nailed to a tree. It is not difficult to see how the story of Isaac, as ancient prophecy about Jesus Christ, could be corrupted into the Greek myth. The constellation Aries was linked to this myth, being a cosmic picture of the ram with the Golden Fleece. Therefore, there is a clear link between Jesus and Aries.

---

[117] Gen 22:13-14
[118] Pseudo-Apollodorus, Bibliotheca 1. 80, http://www.theoi.com/Ther/KriosKhrysomallos.html

In ancient Babylonian texts, Aries was called "the hired man." Astronomy researcher, Gavin White, explains: *"In fact, the name of the 'Hired Man' is a learned pun that needs to be interpreted in two very different ways. At face value the 'Hired Man' refers to the additional farm labourers employed in the spring to bring in the barley harvest. But his name, as a spoken rather than written form, can also be understood as something like 'the Sheep of Atonement'."*[119]

Aries in the Law and the Prophets

The Passover sacrificial lamb carried this prophetic tradition into the Law of Moses. The lamb's blood applied to the doorposts of the home meant that the death angel was forbidden entrance. The fifty-third chapter of Isaiah provided further details about the Lamb provided by God as a sacrifice for sins. Yet, Isaiah prophesied that the Jews would reject God's sacrificial Lamb. He lamented, *"who has believed our report?"* Indeed, the Jews generally did not, and do not, believe Isaiah or the One he prophesied about. *"And we hid, as it were, our faces from Him; He was despised, and we did not esteem Him."* Instead, Isaiah's own people *"considered him stricken by God, smitten by him, and afflicted."* The Jews considered Jesus to be a blasphemer and condemned to death by the Law of Moses. In their eyes, His crucifixion was God's just punishment upon Him for His blasphemy. Isaiah's prophecy states plainly that his own people would not believe his prophecy, and that they would reject the Lamb of God. That Isaiah foretold of this rejection ought to give any modern-day Jew pause. The Jewish interpretation of this prophecy has

---

[119] White, Gavin, The Exaltation System in Babylonian Astrology, http://www.skyscript.co.uk/exaltations.html

been consistently wrong since the time of Jesus. Isaiah said they would get it wrong; and indeed they have. This implies that the Christian interpretation is indeed correct.

Isaiah linked the Lamb of God to the Branch in Virgo's right hand. *"My servant grew up in the LORD's presence like a tender green shoot, sprouting from a root in dry and sterile ground."*[120] The word "Branch" in the prophecies about David's heir literally means "shoot."[121] The shoot in Virgo's right hand, the promised Seed of Abraham, becomes the sacrificial Lamb. *"He was oppressed and He was afflicted, Yet He opened not His mouth; He was led as a lamb to the slaughter, And as a sheep before its shearers is silent, So He opened not His mouth. He was taken from prison and from judgment, And who will declare His generation? For He was cut off from the land of the living; For the transgressions of My people He was stricken. ... Yet it pleased the LORD to bruise Him; He has put Him to grief. When You make His soul an offering for sin, ... He shall see the labor of His soul, and be satisfied. By His knowledge My righteous Servant shall justify many, For He shall bear their iniquities."*[122] John the Baptist pointed to the fulfillment of Isaiah's prophecy, the "Lamb of God." Paul concurred: *"Christ our Passover was sacrificed for us."*[123]

In the Egyptian zodiac of Dendera, the goddess herself (Hathor / Isis) is depicted as the constellation Virgo, standing with the wheat in her hand between Leo and Libra. She is also the life-like image stretched out beside the zodiac. Virgo is a

---

[120] Isaiah 53:2 NLT
[121] Isaiah 11:1; Jeremiah 23:5; Jeremiah 33:15; Zechariah 3:8; Zechariah 6:12
[122] Isaiah 53:7-11
[123] 1 Corinthians 5:7

representation of Sarah, the mother of both the Redeemer and the redeemed. Aries is aligned perfectly with her birth canal. The woman bringing forth the male Child has Aries emerging from her womb.

All of the zodiacal constellations that deal with Israel's history in the Old Testament—Virgo, Libra, Scorpio, Sagittarius, Capricorn, Aquarius, and Pisces—are depicted above her vaginal area. Aries brings the birth of the Branch (shoot) from Sarah's womb. The zodiacal constellations that deal with the New Testament story—Aries, Taurus, Gemini, Cancer, and Leo—are not concealed within her body, but revealed outside. They all follow the birth of Aries, Jesus Christ, the Lamb of God. The signs above her vaginal area were concealed — the "mystery" of which Paul frequently wrote. Aries and the signs that follow are revealed through Aries Himself. Once He was born, the mystery was unsealed and "proclaimed to all nations for the obedience of faith."[124]

---

[124] Romans 16:25-26

MYSTERY of the MAZZAROTH

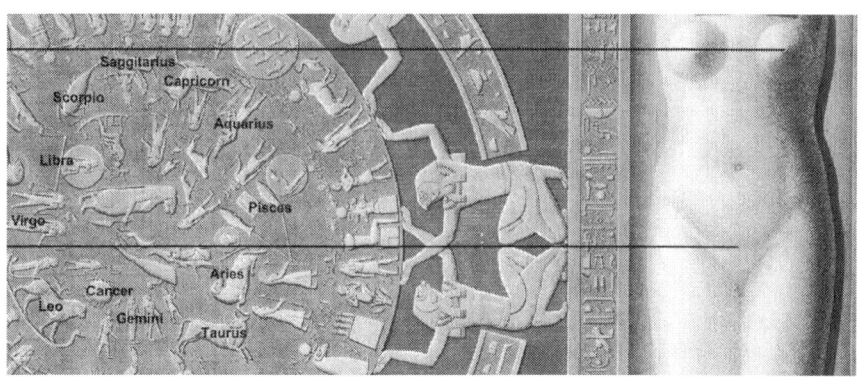

The Sacrifice of Aries

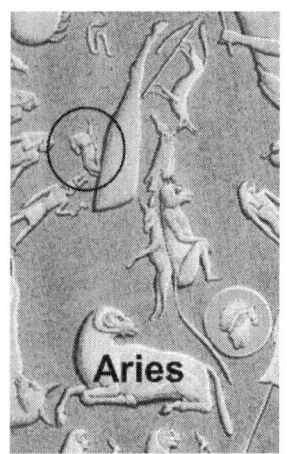

Directly above the head of Aries in the zodiac of Dendera is a severed lamb's leg. Some have tried to identify this severed leg with Ursa Major (Big Dipper), but Ursa Major is above Leo, not Aries. Attached to the severed leg is a miniature icon of Aries (circled). It is apparent that this small icon was intended to identify the severed leg as belonging to Aries, thus indicating that Aries was to be sacrificed.

The Lamb of God was born to die. *"Therefore, when He came into the world, He said: 'Sacrifice and offering You did not desire, But a body You have prepared for Me. In burnt offerings and sacrifices for sin You had no pleasure.' Then I said, 'Behold, I have come—In the volume of the book it is written of Me —To do Your will, O God.' Previously saying, 'Sacrifice and offering, burnt offerings, and offerings for sin You did not desire, nor had pleasure in them' (which are offered according to the law), then He said, 'Behold, I have come to do Your will, O God.' He takes away the first that He may establish the second. By that will we have been sanctified through the offering of the body of Jesus Christ once for all."*[125]

Jesus was Crucified on Passover, with the Sun in Aries

God commanded that the Passover lamb be chosen on the 10th day of the month Nisan. It was to be unblemished, separated from the flock, and held until the 14th. It was on the 10th of Nisan that Jesus rode into Jerusalem on the donkey. The Passover lamb was to be killed in the late afternoon of the 14th and eaten during the night.[126] Since the days on the Jewish calendar begin at sundown, the Passover lamb was actually consumed on the 15th. Jesus was crucified on the 15th shortly after eating the Passover with His disciples. As the Lamb of God hung on the cross, Passover lamb was in His stomach.

---

[125] Heb 10:5-10
[126] Exodus 12:1-11

At noon the sun became completely dark and remained dark for three hours. The cause of the darkness was not merely the sun being obscured by dark clouds. Luke tells us: *"And it was already about the sixth hour, and darkness came over the whole land till the ninth hour **at the defaulting of the sun**."*[127] The effect would be similar to a total solar eclipse.[128] The sky would become as dark as midnight. The stars and constellations would be seen clearly, since the sun's light would not be passing through the atmosphere to illuminate it. As people looked up at the sky in horror, they would have observed the constellation Aries directly overhead where the noon sun had been. This terrifying scene continued until Jesus expired at three o'clock. Someone standing close on the east side of the cross, facing the cross looking west, would have observed Aries slowly sinking head first down behind Jesus' head as those three hours passed.

---

[127] Luke 24:44-45 CLV

[128] The cause of the darkness could not have been a solar eclipse, since on Passover the earth is always between the moon and the sun. Only lunar eclipses are possible on Passover.

Chapter 11
Taurus
The Apostolic Mission

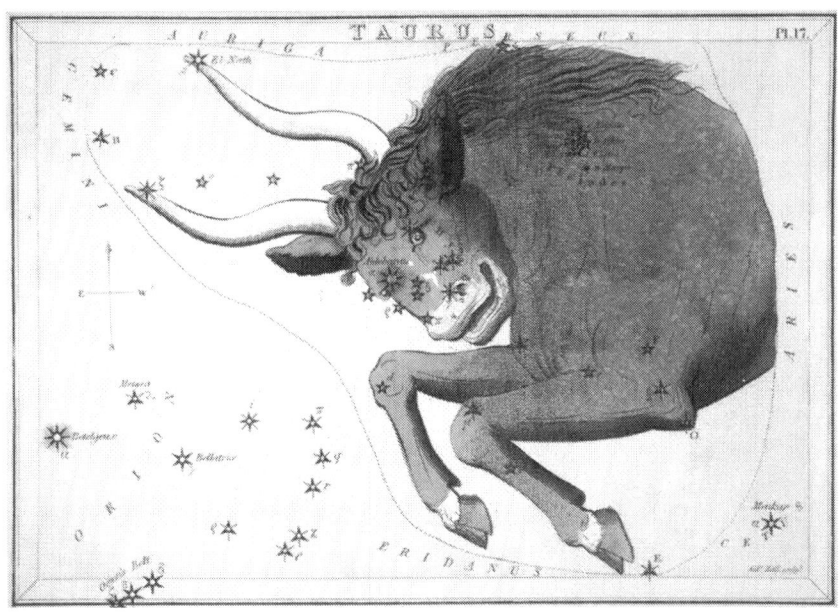

1 Corinthians 9:2, 9-13
2 If I am not an apostle to others, yet doubtless I am to you. For you are the seal of my apostleship in the Lord. ...
9 For it is written in the law of Moses, "You shall not muzzle an <u>ox</u> while it treads out the grain." Is it <u>oxen</u> God is concerned about? 10 Or does He say it altogether for our sakes? For our sakes, no doubt, this is written, that he who plows should plow in hope, and he who threshes in hope should be partaker of his hope. 11 If we have sown spiritual

things for you, is it a great thing if we reap your material things? 12 If others are partakers of this right over you, are we not even more? Nevertheless we have not used this right, but endure all things lest we hinder the gospel of Christ.

The Apostle Paul likened himself and his fellow Apostles to oxen pulling a plow and powering a threshing mill. Pulling the plow is preaching the Gospel of Jesus Christ. Driving the threshing mill, grinding the raw wheat into flour that can be used in making bread, refers to the rest of their job—*"teaching them to observe all things that I have commanded you."*[129] No doubt Paul borrowed these ox metaphors from Jesus' own words: *"Take My yoke upon you ... for My yoke is easy and My burden is light."*[130]

Paul indicated that the command in the Law of Moses, *"You shall not muzzle an ox while it treads out the grain,"* was not written by Moses primarily because God cares about oxen. Rather, this command was given to Israel as a prophecy of the Apostolic ministry. Those who have dedicated their lives to pulling Jesus' plow or powering His grinding mill are to have their needs met from their ministry, taking some of the fruit of their labor for their own needs. This applies to full-time preachers and teachers.

Some have seen in Taurus a charging bull. Taurus is not a charging bull, but an ox straining as he pulls a very heavy load. An ox is a domesticated bull, trained since he was a calf to pull heavy loads and obey the commands of his driver.

---

[129] Matthew 28:18-20
[130] Matt 11:29-30

This is the perfect representation of the Apostolic ministry. It was the job of the Apostles to proclaim to all the nations the "revelation of the mystery."[131]

The Twelve Oxen in Solomon's Temple
The Temple of Solomon was designed by God to provide the same kind of symbolic imagery as the constellations. Its layout and furnishings all have symbolic meaning pointing to the Gospel of Jesus Christ. The bronze altar of sacrifice just inside the eastern gate, where the blood of the sacrificial animals flowed, and where their carcasses were burned, symbolized the cross of Jesus Christ. The Lamb of God was sacrificed for the sins of all mankind. The next structure was an enormous bronze bowl supported by twelve cast bronze oxen, three facing east, three facing west, three facing north, and three facing south.

> *2 Chron. 4:2-4*
> *2 Then he made the Sea of cast bronze, ten cubits from one brim to the other; it was completely round. Its height was five cubits, and a line of thirty cubits measured its circumference.*
> *3 And under it was the likeness of oxen encircling it all around, ten to a cubit, all the way around the Sea. The oxen were cast in two rows, when it was cast.*
> *4* <u>***It stood on twelve oxen: three looking toward the north, three looking toward the west, three looking toward the south, and three looking toward the east;***</u>

---

[131] Luke 24:44-49; Romans 16:25-26; 1 Corinthians 2:6-13; Ephesians 3:1-7

the Sea was set upon them, and all their back parts pointed inward.

The twelve oxen represent the twelve Apostles. That they are facing the four points of the compass indicates their mission to carrying the Gospel to all the nations. The three hundred small oxen cast all around the rim of the reservoir represent all those who follow in the footsteps of the Apostles, taking the Great Commission as their mission. The enormous reservoir of water on the backs of the twelve oxen represents the cleansing waters of baptism through which they make disciples of all the nations. In Solomon's Temple, the priests bathed in this water before they could enter the Temple to perform their sacred service. So too, the repentant sinner must come to the altar of sacrifice—the cross—and enter the waters of baptism before he is fit to enter the presence of God. Taurus is simply an abbreviated form of the symbol of Solomon's bronze laver, which represents the Apostolic ministry.

The Constellation Orion
Orion is not part of the zodiac. It lies just below the ecliptic between Gemini and Taurus. Yet, Orion is as old as any of the other constellations. It is named in Job, the oldest book of the Bible. *"Can you bind the cluster of the Pleiades, Or loose the belt of Orion? Can you bring out Mazzaroth in its season?"*[132] Job lived about the time of Abraham, indicating that this constellation was known in Abraham's day, about 2000 BC.

---

[132] Job 38:31-32

Orion is pictured as a hunter attacking Taurus with a huge bronze club. That Orion is the opponent of the "heavenly bull" is consistent in all mythologies.

According to the Greek myth, Scorpio's sting is said to have caused Orion's death. As we observed in the third chapter, the scorpion's sting is God's rejection demanded by the Law of Moses in response to Israel's disobedience. It was first manifest in the wilderness, when God rejected Israel and would not allow that generation to enter the land. Orion represents the apostates of Israel, having been stung by the scorpion, rejected by God, yet still opposing and persecuting the Apostles as they labored to pull the plow of Christ.

It is no coincidence that the Hebrew word for "Orion" in Job 9:9, Job 38:31, and Amos 5:8, literally means "fat," and figuratively means "fool, stupid fellow, dullard, simpleton, arrogant one."[133] His name brings to mind the Song of Moses which God commanded Moses to teach to the Israelites before entering the Promised Land.

---

[133] Strong's Concordance Hebrew Lexicon #3684 - 3685

Deuteronomy 32:11-21

11 As an eagle stirs up its nest, Hovers over its young, Spreading out its wings, taking them up, Carrying them on its wings, 12 So the LORD alone led him, And there was no foreign god with him. 13 "He made him ride in the heights of the earth, That he might eat the produce of the fields; He made him draw honey from the rock, And oil from the flinty rock; 14 Curds from the cattle, and milk of the flock, With fat of lambs; And rams of the breed of Bashan, and goats, With the choicest wheat; And you drank wine, the blood of the grapes.

15 "But Jeshurun[134] grew fat and kicked; You grew fat, you grew thick, You are obese! Then he forsook God who made him, And scornfully esteemed the Rock of his salvation.

16 They provoked Him to jealousy with foreign gods; With abominations they provoked Him to anger. 17 They sacrificed to demons, not to God, To gods they did not know, To new gods, new arrivals That your fathers did not fear. 18 Of the Rock who begot you, you are unmindful, And have forgotten the God who fathered you.

19 "And when the LORD saw it, He spurned them, Because of the provocation of His sons and His daughters. 20 And He said: 'I will hide My face from them, I will see what their end will be, For they are a perverse generation, Children in whom is no faith. 21 They have provoked Me to jealousy by what is not God; They have moved Me to anger by their foolish idols. **<u>But I will provoke them to jealousy by those who are not a nation; I will move them to anger by a foolish nation</u>**.

---

[134] "Jeshurun" means "the one having been beloved," referring to God's having called Israel out of slavery.

MYSTERY of the MAZZAROTH

The song of Moses is a song about the unfaithful majority of Israel, pictured in the sky as Orion, the fat one, the fool, always opposing God. Yet, the song of Moses does not end here. It goes on to speak of God's eventual restoration of Israel. God will *"provoke them to jealousy by those who are not a nation; I will move them to anger by a foolish nation."* The Apostle Paul referenced this very statement in the eleventh chapter of Romans. *"I say then, have they stumbled that they should fall? Certainly not! But through their fall, to provoke them to jealousy, salvation has come to the Gentiles. Now if their fall is riches for the world, and their failure riches for the Gentiles, how much more their fullness! ... For if their being cast away is the reconciling of the world, what will their acceptance be but life from the dead?"*[135]

Just as Orion opposes Taurus, raising his bronze club to strike down the plowing ox, so too did unbelieving Israel oppose and strike the Apostles in a failed attempt to stop the spread of the Gospel of Jesus Christ.

The Greek myth of Orion not only spoke of his having been stung by Scorpio, but also his total blindness and the eventual restoration of his sight which would be received at the "dawn."

> *"On the island of Chios, Orion wooed Merope, daughter of King Oenopion, apparently without much success, for one night while fortified with wine he tried to ravish her. In punishment, Oenopion put out Orion's eyes and banished him from the island. Orion headed north to the island of*

---

[135] Romans 11:11-15

Lemnos where Hephaestus had his forge. Hephaestus took pity on the blind Orion and offered one of his assistants, Cedalion, to act as his eyes. Hoisting the youth on his shoulders, Orion headed east towards the sunrise, which an oracle had told him would restore his sight. As the sun's healing rays fell on his sightless eyes at dawn, Orion's vision was miraculously restored."[136]

This myth is clearly a corruption of ancient oral prophecy regarding Israel's blindness and eventual restoration. Orion's vision will one day be miraculously restored at the Dawn of the Seventh Day, Christ's Kingdom. The Apostle Paul described it this way:

> Rom 11:25-29
> *25 For I do not desire, brethren, that you should be ignorant of this mystery, lest you should be wise in your own opinion, that blindness in part has happened to Israel until the fullness of the Gentiles has come in.*
> *26 And so all Israel will be saved, as it is written: "The Deliverer will come out of Zion, And He will turn away ungodliness from Jacob; 27 For this is My covenant with them, When I take away their sins."*
> *28 Concerning the gospel they are enemies for your sake, but concerning the election they are beloved for the sake of the fathers. 29 For the gifts and the calling of God are irrevocable.*

---

[136] Ridpath, Ian, Star Tales, Orion, http://www.ianridpath.com/startales/orion.htm

The second coming of Jesus Christ to restore His creation is called the sunrise.[137] This is when blind Orion will finally receive his sight.

Orion's belt is the brightest, most recognizable feature of the night sky. Orion's belt is mentioned in Job in the following words: *"Can you bind the cluster of the Pleiades, Or loose the belt of Orion?"*[138] The obvious answer to God's rhetorical question is, no: no one can loose Orion's belt. Why? Because Orion's belt is God's unbreakable promise to Abraham! This is why Paul wrote above, *"And so all Israel will be saved, as it is written: 'The Deliverer will come out of Zion, And He will turn away ungodliness from Jacob; For this is My covenant with them, When I take away their sins.' Concerning the gospel they are enemies for your sake, but concerning the election they are beloved for the sake of the fathers. For the gifts and the calling of God are irrevocable."*

There is coming a day of repentance for national Israel. It will be a bitter day. In the Revelation, John writes: *"Behold, He is coming with clouds, and every eye will see Him, even they who pierced Him. And all the tribes of the earth will mourn because of Him. Even so, Amen."*[139] Zechariah prophesied of this repentance also.

> *Zech. 12:10-11*
> *10 "And I will pour on the house of David and on the inhabitants of Jerusalem the Spirit of grace and supplication; then they will look on Me whom they pierced. Yes, they will*

---

[137] Malachi 4:2; 2 Peter 1:19
[138] Job 38:31
[139] Revelation 1:7

mourn for Him as one mourns for his only son, and grieve for Him as one grieves for a firstborn. 11 In that day there shall be a great mourning in Jerusalem, like the mourning at Hadad Rimmon in the plain of Megiddo.

The Pleiades

Within the left shoulder of Taurus is a tight cluster of stars called the Pleiades, also mentioned in Job. It is one of two tight star clusters within the zodiac constellations visible to the naked eye. The other is in Cancer.

NASA photo of the Pleiades

The Pleiades were known anciently as "the seven sisters." The Greek myth states that Zeus turned the seven sisters into a flock of seven doves, and placed them in the constellation Taurus. *"According to other authorities, the name comes from the*

Greek word peleiades, meaning 'flock of doves'."[140] Most people can see only six of the stars with the naked eye. Those with exceptional eyesight can see seven or even more.

In the Bible, the dove is a symbol for the Holy Spirit. The Gospels tell us that the Holy Spirit descended in the form of a dove upon Jesus at His baptism, indicating God's empowerment to accomplish His mission on earth. The Holy Spirit has seven aspects according to Isaiah. This seven-fold Spirit of God will empower the "Branch" from David's seed, the Messiah, to reign in His Kingdom.

> *Isaiah 11:1-4*
> *1 There shall come forth a Rod from the stem of Jesse, And a Branch shall grow out of his roots. 2 The Spirit of the LORD shall rest upon Him, The Spirit of wisdom and understanding, The Spirit of counsel and might, The Spirit of knowledge and of the fear of the LORD.*
> *3 His delight is in the fear of the LORD, And He shall not judge by the sight of His eyes, Nor decide by the hearing of His ears; 4 But with righteousness He shall judge the poor, And decide with equity for the meek of the earth; He shall strike the earth with the rod of His mouth, And with the breath of His lips He shall slay the wicked."*

The Spirit of God is referred to as "seven Spirits" sent to assist Zerubbabel in rebuilding the second Temple.[141] They are also

---

[140] Ridpath, Ian, Star Tales, Taurus Part II, http://www.ianridpath.com/startales/taurus2.htm
[141] Zechariah 3:9

represented as "seven eyes" in the same passage.[142] Jesus Himself said that He possessed the seven-fold Spirit of God prophesied by Isaiah to empower the Messiah. *"These things says He who has the seven Spirits of God."*[143] In his vision of heaven, John also observed *"in the midst of the elders, stood a Lamb as though it had been slain, having seven horns **and seven eyes, which are the seven Spirits of God** sent out into all the earth."*[144] It is apparent that the Pleiades represent the empowerment of the seven-fold Spirit: the Spirit of Jehovah,[145] the spirit of wisdom, the spirit of understanding, the spirit of counsel, the spirit of might, the spirit of knowledge, and the spirit of the fear of Jehovah.

That the Pleiades is perched on the shoulder of Taurus is to be expected, since Jesus explained to His Apostles the necessity of the Holy Spirit's empowerment to complete their mission on His behalf.

> *Acts 1:6-8*
> *6 Therefore, when they had come together, they asked Him, saying, "Lord, will You at this time restore the kingdom to Israel?"*
> *7 And He said to them, "It is not for you to know times or seasons which the Father has put in His own authority. 8 But you shall receive power when the Holy Spirit has come*

---

[142] Zechariah 4:10
[143] Revelation 3:1
[144] Rev 5:6
[145] Yahveh (sometimes pronounced, "Jehovah") is the Hebrew name of God in the OT.

upon you; and you shall be witnesses to Me in Jerusalem, and in all Judea and Samaria, and to the end of the earth."

The Pleiades perched on the shoulder of Taurus is the promise of the Holy Spirit to Jesus' Apostles, empowering them to carry the waters of baptism to all the nations, to plow the hearts of men, plant the Gospel, and thresh the wheat that is produced. Jesus made the promise of the Spirit to His disciples the night before His crucifixion.[146] Three days later He rose from the dead. He then spent the next forty days teaching them concerning His coming Kingdom.[147] On the fortieth day, Jesus ascended to heaven.

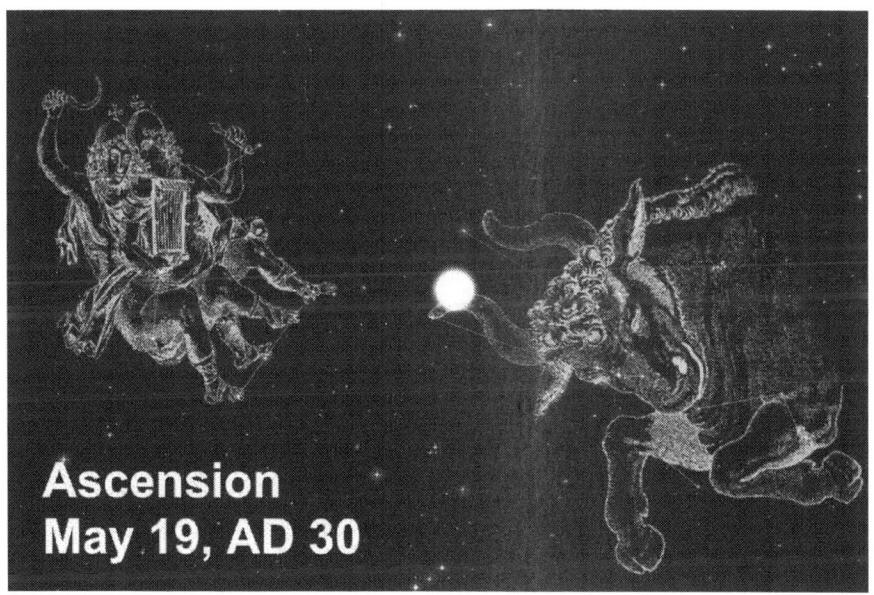

Ascension
May 19, AD 30

---

[146] John 14:16, 26; John 15:26-27; John 16:7-15
[147] Acts 1:3

MYSTERY of the MAZZAROTH

When Jesus was crucified, the sun was in the heart of Aries. During the forty days between His resurrection and ascension, while He gave His Apostles their final training, the sun slowly progressed through Taurus. On the day of His ascension, the sun was leaving the tip of Taurus' horn. As the sun left Taurus, the Son of God left His team of oxen, ascending to the right hand of the Father to wait until their job of plowing and threshing was completed.

Chapter 12
Gemini
Gentiles Joined to Abraham's Seed

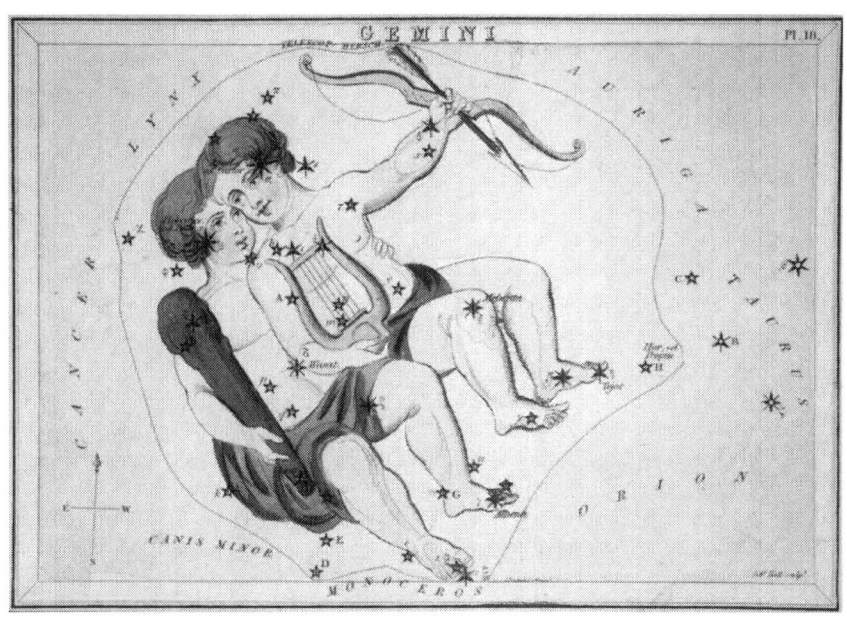

Eph 3:1-6
1 For this reason I, Paul, the prisoner of Christ Jesus for you Gentiles—2 if indeed you have heard of the dispensation of the grace of God which was given to me for you, 3 how that by revelation He made known to me the mystery (as I have briefly written already, 4 by which, when you read, you may understand my knowledge in the mystery of Christ), 5 which in other ages was not made known to the sons of men, as it has now been revealed by the Spirit to His holy apostles and

prophets: 6 that the Gentiles should be fellow heirs, of the same body, and partakers of His promise in Christ through the gospel."

The constellation Gemini pictures twins embracing. The twin on the right represents the believing remnant of Israel to which the Apostles belonged. They were the natural heirs to the promises of Abraham and to the New Covenant prophesied by Jeremiah. This twin holds an arrow and a lyre. The arrow is for hunting the souls of men – the Great Commission – and the lyre is for the worship of the Lamb (Aries) through the Psalms of David.

The twin on the left represents the Gentiles, adopted into Israel by being baptized into Jesus Christ, having become heirs of the promises along with Abraham's natural sons. This twin holds a sickle, represented as a club in some drawings. The sickle also represents the Great Commission.

When Jesus commissioned His Apostles after His resurrection, He instructed them to begin preaching to the Jews first, then the Samaritans and Gentiles. But, He also told them to wait in Jerusalem for the promised Holy Spirit before they began their mission.

> *Acts 1:4-8*
> *4 And being assembled together with them, He commanded them not to depart from Jerusalem, but to wait for the Promise of the Father, "which," He said, "you have heard from Me; 5 for John truly baptized with water, but you shall be baptized with the Holy Spirit not many days from now."*

> *6 Therefore, when they had come together, they asked Him, saying, "Lord, will You at this time restore the kingdom to Israel?"*
>
> *7 And He said to them, "It is not for you to know times or seasons which the Father has put in His own authority. 8 But you shall receive power when the Holy Spirit has come upon you; and you shall be witnesses to Me in Jerusalem, and in all Judea and Samaria, and to the end of the earth."*

The Apostles waited in the upper room for ten more days after Jesus ascended, not knowing exactly when the Holy Spirit might come. No doubt they noticed that Jesus was crucified on the Passover and what that signified in light of John the Baptist's announcement that Jesus was the "Lamb of God."[148] They were also aware that His resurrection occurred on the feast of Firstfruits, when the token sheaf was waved before the Lord symbolizing the whole harvest yet to come, and how it signified Jesus' resurrection being "the firstfruits of those who sleep."[149] They knew that the feast of Pentecost was approaching and that Jewish travelers from all over the Roman Empire were slowly filling the city for the upcoming festivities. They were aware of the ceremonies that would take place at the Temple on the fiftieth day, with the high priest waving the two "wave loaves" of baked bread from east to west before the Lord.[150] Yet they probably did not yet understand the significance of the two wave loaves as symbols representing the same things the Gemini twins represent. Nor did they understand the symbolism of their

---

[148] 1 Corinthians 5:7
[149] 1 Corinthians 15:20,23
[150] Lev. 23:16-17

being waved from east to west by the priest, showing the spread of the Gospel.

So, they waited patiently until the fiftieth day came—the Jewish Feast of Pentecost. Suddenly, the Holy Spirit arrived in dramatic fashion, filling each of them with the power to accomplish their mission. Yet something else was happening during their wait. A celestial clock had been ticking down those ten days. The sun had left the tip of Taurus' horn when Jesus ascended, and was slowly moving to the foot of the right twin. On the Day of Pentecost, the sun moved into Gemini, eclipsing the star on the right foot of the right twin. It was time to begin preaching the Gospel to the Jews.

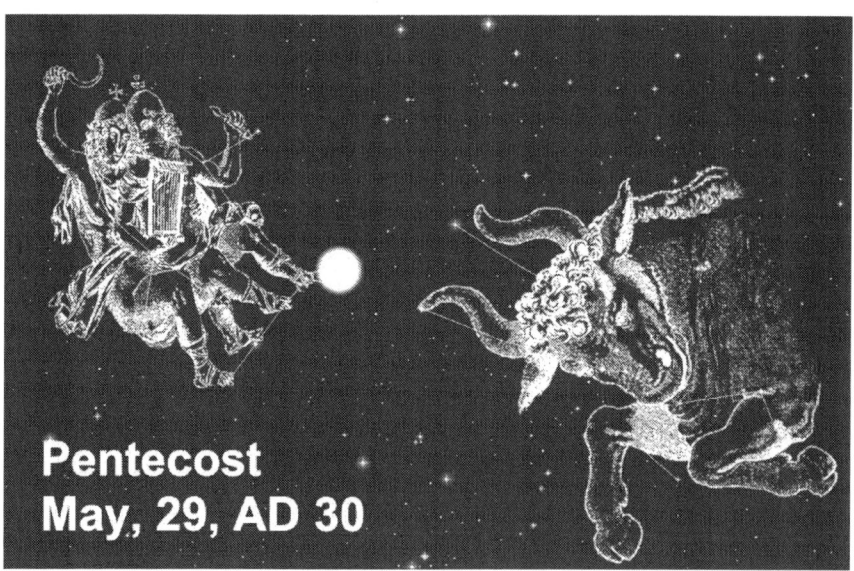

Pentecost
May, 29, AD 30

The Roman names of the twins are Castor and Pollux. Castor is on the right holding the lyre, representing believing Israel. Pollux is on the left, representing believing Gentiles. Some

Greek myths claimed that the twins' mother slept with both her husband and Zeus on the same night, one having a human father and the other a god for a father. Perhaps this tale grew from ancient prophecy of Israel being reckoned as sons of God when He called them out of Egypt.[151]

Peter understood from Jesus' commission, that they must preach the Gospel beginning in Jerusalem, and that the Jews had priority. They were the natural descendants of Abraham. On the Day of Pentecost, Peter's first sermon resulted in three thousand conversions. His sermon was remarkable, particularly in the way he handled the Old Testament prophecies of Jesus Christ and His resurrection, demonstrating the power of the Holy Spirit. His second sermon was just as remarkable.

> *Acts 3:13-26*
> *13 The God of Abraham, Isaac, and Jacob, the God of our fathers, glorified His Servant Jesus, whom you delivered up and denied in the presence of Pilate, when he was determined to let Him go. 14 But you denied the Holy One and the Just, and asked for a murderer to be granted to you, 15 and killed the Prince of life, whom God raised from the dead, of which we are witnesses.*
> *16 And His name, through faith in His name, has made this man strong, whom you see and know. Yes, the faith which comes through Him has given him this perfect soundness in the presence of you all.*

---

[151] Exodus 4:22

> *17 "Yet now, brethren, I know that you did it in ignorance, as did also your rulers.*
> *18 But those things which God foretold by the mouth of all His prophets, that the Christ would suffer, He has thus fulfilled.*
> *19 Repent therefore and be converted, that your sins may be blotted out, so that times of refreshing may come from the presence of the Lord, 20 and that He may send Jesus Christ, who was preached to you before, 21 whom heaven must receive until the times of restoration of all things, which God has spoken by the mouth of all His holy prophets since the world began.*
> *22 For Moses truly said to the fathers, 'The LORD your God will raise up for you a Prophet like me from your brethren. Him you shall hear in all things, whatever He says to you. 23 And it shall be that every soul who will not hear that Prophet shall be utterly destroyed from among the people.'*
> *24 Yes, and all the prophets, from Samuel and those who follow, as many as have spoken, have also foretold these days.*
> *25 You are sons of the prophets, and of the covenant which God made with our fathers, saying to Abraham, 'And in your seed all the families of the earth shall be blessed.' 26* **To you first***, God, having raised up His Servant Jesus, sent Him to bless you, in turning away every one of you from your iniquities."*

Verse 25 shows the special relationship the Jews had to the Gospel of Jesus Christ. His hearers were the *"sons of the prophets, and of the covenant which God made with our fathers."* That covenant indicated that all nations would be blessed through Abraham's Seed. That "Seed" was one person, Jesus

Christ. Yet, knowing that the Apostolic mission meant bringing the inheritance of Abraham to all the heathen nations, Peter told them that God sent Jesus to bless the Jews first before extending the blessing to the Gentiles, as He promised Abraham. Peter encouraged them not to squander their preferential treatment.

Paul had the same attitude. When writing to the Romans, three times he indicated the Gospel was *"to the Jew first, and also to the Greek."*[152] When Paul went from city to city preaching the Gospel, he always went to the synagogue first. Only when he was rejected in the synagogue did he turn his attention to the Gentiles.[153] Just as Peter understood the Jewish priority from Jesus' command, so too did Paul understand it from Jesus' commission to him on the Damascus road.

> *Acts 26:16-18*
> *16 But rise and stand on your feet; for I have appeared to you for this purpose, to make you a minister and a witness both of the things which you have seen and of the things which I will yet reveal to you.*
> *17 I will deliver you from the Jewish people, as well as from the Gentiles, to whom I now send you, 18 to open their eyes, in order to turn them from darkness to light, and from the power of Satan to God, that they may receive forgiveness of sins and* **an inheritance among those who are sanctified by faith in Me**.*'*

---

[152] Romans 1:16 & 2:9-10
[153] Acts 13:15; Acts 14:1; Acts 17:1-2; Acts 17:10; Acts 17:16-17; Acts 18:4; Acts 19:8; Acts 28:17

The Gentiles were to be added to a body of redeemed men that already existed—redeemed Jews. Jesus did not come to start a new religion. He came to fulfill the prophecies to Israel. The disciples and other Jews who received the Gospel from all twelve tribes of Israel entered into the New Covenant prophesied by Jeremiah and inaugurated by Christ at His crucifixion.[154] The message proclaimed by Jesus' Apostles was the coming of a New Covenant which makes possible the blessings of the Abrahamic Covenant, releasing Israel from the condemnation of the Law and adopting the Gentiles into the Abrahamic Covenant as sons of Abraham, co-heirs with Jesus Christ.

While Paul's primary assignment was to proclaim the Gospel among the Gentiles, his heart was with his Jewish brothers who refused the Messiah of Israel. *"I tell the truth in Christ, I am not lying, my conscience also bearing me witness in the Holy Spirit, that I have great sorrow and continual grief in my heart. For I could wish that I myself were accursed from Christ for my brethren, my countrymen according to the flesh, who are Israelites, to whom pertain the adoption, the glory, the covenants, the giving of the law, the service of God, and the promises; of whom are the fathers and from whom, according to the flesh, Christ came, who is over all, the eternally blessed God. Amen."*[155] Again, Paul writes: *"Brethren, my heart's desire and prayer to God for Israel is that they may be saved. For I bear them witness that they have a zeal for God, but not according to knowledge. For they being ignorant of God's righteousness, and seeking to establish their own righteousness,*

---

[154] Matthew 26:26-29; 2 Corinthians 3:6; Hebrews 8:13; Hebrews 9:15; Hebrews 12:24
[155] Romans 9:1-5

have not submitted to the righteousness of God. For Christ is the end of the law for righteousness to everyone who believes."[156]

Paul rejoiced in the fact that a significant number of his brethren embraced the New Covenant. Just as at Kadesh Barnea, when God pronounced judgment on Israel, not all were destroyed. God had not cast away the whole nation because of unbelief, but would fulfill His promise to Abraham through a small remnant. *"I say then, has God cast away His people? Certainly not! For I also am an Israelite, of the seed of Abraham, of the tribe of Benjamin. God has not cast away His people whom He foreknew. Or do you not know what the Scripture says of Elijah, how he pleads with God against Israel, saying, "LORD, they have killed Your prophets and torn down Your altars, and I alone am left, and they seek my life"? But what does the divine response say to him? "I have reserved for Myself seven thousand men who have not bowed the knee to Baal." Even so then, at this present time there is a remnant according to the election of grace."*[157]

Paul's Ministry of Reconciliation

The inclusion of the Gentiles within Abraham's seed was not a novel idea. The prophets had declared it long ago. Paul was keenly aware of these prophecies as he labored in his mission. In encouraging the unity of the church in Rome (which consisted of both Jews and Gentiles), Paul cited as his authority several Old Testament prophecies which foretold the Gentiles' participation in the promises to Israel. *"Therefore receive one another, just as Christ also received us, to the glory of God. Now I say that Jesus Christ has become a servant to the*

---

[156] Romans 10:1-4
[157] Romans 11:1-5

circumcision for the truth of God, to confirm the promises made to the fathers, and that the Gentiles might glorify God for His mercy, as it is written: 'For this reason I will confess to You among the Gentiles, And sing to Your name.' And again he says: 'Rejoice, O Gentiles, with His people!' And again: 'Praise the LORD, all you Gentiles! Laud Him, all you peoples!' And again, Isaiah says: 'There shall be a root of Jesse; And He who shall rise to reign over the Gentiles, In Him the Gentiles shall hope.'"[158]

The Epistle to the Ephesians stresses this unity of Jew and Gentile in the Abrahamic Covenant through Jesus Christ. Like no other passage, this one best emphasizes the spirit embodied in the sign of Gemini.

> *Eph. 2:11-22*
> *11 Therefore remember that you, once Gentiles in the flesh — who are called Uncircumcision by what is called the Circumcision made in the flesh by hands — 12 that at that time you were without Christ, being aliens from the commonwealth of Israel and strangers from the covenants of promise, having no hope and without God in the world.*
> *13 But now in Christ Jesus you who once were far off have been brought near by the blood of Christ.*
> *14 For He Himself is our peace, who has made both one, and has broken down the middle wall of separation, 15 having abolished in His flesh the enmity, that is, the law of commandments contained in ordinances, so as to create in Himself one new man from the two, thus making peace,*

---
[158] Romans 15:7-12

16 and that He might reconcile them both to God in one body through the cross, thereby putting to death the enmity.
17 And He came and preached peace to you who were afar off and to those who were near.
18 For through Him we both have access by one Spirit to the Father.
19 Now, therefore, you are no longer strangers and foreigners, but fellow citizens with the saints and members of the household of God, 20 having been built on the foundation of the apostles and prophets, Jesus Christ Himself being the chief cornerstone, 21 in whom the whole building, being fitted together, grows into a holy temple in the Lord, 22 in whom you also are being built together for a dwelling place of God in the Spirit.

Paul's Mission Aboard the "Gemini"

Paul had a deep desire to travel to Rome. He expressed this desire in his Epistle to the Romans.[159] He desperately wanted to visit the capitol of the empire. "All roads lead to Rome" was a well-known expression, and for good reason. At the time, it was literally true. The Roman Empire had built roads from Rome to the farthest reaches of the empire for trade as well as moving the army. Rome was the world's hub of commerce. If Paul could develop the church in Rome into a mission-minded institution, he no doubt would see the Gospel spreading along all of the Roman trade routes throughout the whole empire, carried by Christian merchants.

---

[159] Romans 1:8-13; Romans 15:22-24

When Paul was arrested during his last visit to Jerusalem, Jesus appeared to him in a vision telling him that he must bear witness of the Gospel in Rome also.[160] Paul's defense at his trials did not go well by human standards and he was forced to appeal to Caesar. This guaranteed him a trip to Rome. Paul was determined to use his imprisonment at Rome to further the Gospel, both among the Jews as well as the Gentiles.[161]

On his trip to Rome under Roman guard, Paul traveled on three different ships. The first ship took him from Caesarea to Lycia, with Luke accompanying him. From there they were put on an Alexandrian ship which sailed against Paul's warning that disaster awaited. Just as Paul predicted, they were shipwrecked in a violent storm. Paul and Luke ended up on the island of Malta with his Roman guards, where they sat out the winter. When winter ended, Paul and Luke were placed on another Roman merchant ship from Alexandria heading for Rome. Luke recorded a very curious detail about this ship, a detail he had omitted regarding the other two ships. *"After three months we sailed in an Alexandrian ship **whose figurehead was the Twin Brothers**, which had wintered at the island."*[162]

What a coincidence! After being shipwrecked and washed ashore on this island, Paul and Luke found themselves on an Alexandrian merchant ship that seemingly had been waiting there for them – the "Gemini" – to carry them safely to Rome.

---

[160] Acts 23:11
[161] Acts 28:17-31
[162] Acts 28:11

MYSTERY of the MAZZAROTH

Why would Luke record the figurehead of this ship and not the other two? The Roman merchant ships of the time typically had figureheads – usually a very large swan facing rearward at the stern. But this ship was unique. Instead of the usual swan, there were the looming figures of Castor and Pollux embracing each other on the stern of the ship. This certainly caught Luke's eye, and perhaps was the subject of conversation between Paul and his companion as they sailed for Rome. Perhaps Paul's mission to Rome to bring the Gospel to the whole Roman Empire, thereby making the Gentiles co-heirs with the Jews, was something Paul and Luke saw in the image of Gemini. How appropriate it was for Paul's vessel to display the sign of Gemini while carrying to the capital of the Gentile world the very Apostle charged with uniting Jew and Gentile in Christ.

MYSTERY of the MAZZAROTH

Chapter 13
Cancer
The Great Tribulation

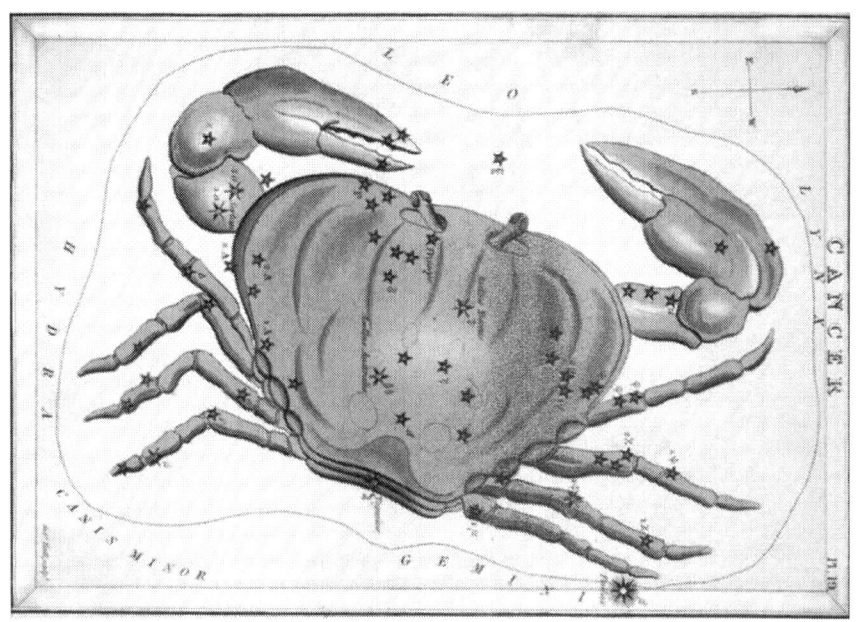

2 Thess. 2:1-6

1 Now, brethren, concerning the coming of our Lord Jesus Christ and our gathering together to Him, we ask you, 2 not to be soon shaken in mind or troubled, either by spirit or by word or by letter, as if from us, as though the day of Christ had come.

3 Let no one deceive you by any means; for that Day will not come unless the falling away comes first, and the man of sin is revealed, the son of perdition, 4 who opposes and exalts

himself above all that is called God or that is worshiped, so that he sits as God in the temple of God, showing himself that he is God.
5 Do you not remember that when I was still with you I told you these things? 6 And now you know what is restraining, that he may be revealed in his own time.

The crab is an unclean animal, included among the "creeping things" (vermin). There are no direct references to the crab in Scripture. However, we do find one indirect reference.

Jude 1:3-4
*3 Beloved, while I was very diligent to write to you concerning our common salvation, I found it necessary to write to you exhorting you to contend earnestly for the faith which was once for all delivered to the saints. 4 For certain men have **crept in** unnoticed, who long ago were marked out for this condemnation, ungodly men, who turn the grace of our God into lewdness and deny the only Lord God and our Lord Jesus Christ.*

This passage is a warning against the false teachers that John called, "antichrists,"[163] who had "crept" into the local Christian communities unnoticed. The Greek verb rendered "crept in" is "παραεισδυνω," and appears only here in the Bible. It literally means "entered sideways."[164] Figuratively, the term implies gaining entrance by stealth and deception. Crabs do not walk forward, but sideways, and provide a

---
[163] 1 John 2:18-23
[164] para = to the side; eis = proceed to a destination; duno = to sink, settle, or enter

perfect picture of Jude's point. It seems he intended to use the crab as a metaphor for "antichrists" who had crept into the churches "sideways" through deceit and subterfuge.

Jesus warned His disciples in the Olivet Discourse that a time of trouble was coming before He would reign as King. During this time there would be many "false christs." He gave His disciples a series of signs to watch for that would precede His coming, including a "falling away" from the Faith by many of His followers[165] and the "abomination of desolation."[166] This will be the defiling of the Temple in Jerusalem by the principle "false Christ" whom John called "the Antichrist,"[167] also prophesied in the last chapter of Daniel.

As Jesus sent these men to the ends of the earth, He told them to teach new converts "to observe all things whatsoever I have commanded you."[168] This included the command to watch for the signs He said would precede His coming.

> *Mark 13:24-37*
> *24 "But in those days, after that tribulation, the sun will be darkened, and the moon will not give its light; 25 the stars of heaven will fall, and the powers in the heavens will be shaken. 26 Then they will see the Son of Man coming in the clouds with great power and glory. 27 And then He will send His angels, and gather together His elect from the four*

---

[165] Matthew 24:9-14
[166] Matthew 24:15
[167] 1 John 2:18
[168] Matthew 28:18-20

winds, from the farthest part of earth to the farthest part of heaven.
28 "Now learn this parable from the fig tree: When its branch has already become tender, and puts forth leaves, you know that summer is near. 29 So you also, when you see these things happening, know that it is near—at the doors! 30 Assuredly, I say to you, this generation will by no means pass away till all these things take place. 31 Heaven and earth will pass away, but My words will by no means pass away.
32 "But of that day and hour no one knows, not even the angels in heaven, nor the Son, but only the Father.
33 Take heed, watch and pray; for you do not know when the time is.
34 It is like a man going to a far country, who left his house and gave authority to his servants, and to each his work, and commanded the doorkeeper to watch.
35 Watch therefore, for you do not know when the master of the house is coming—in the evening, at midnight, at the crowing of the rooster, or in the morning— 36 lest, coming suddenly, he find you sleeping. 37 ***And what I say to you, I say to all: Watch!"***

The last statement in verse 37 was meant to stress to the disciples the necessity of teaching new Christian converts to be watching for the signs of Jesus' coming "after the tribulation." Some of the signs occur during the tribulation, including the "falling away" of many believers and the "abomination of desolation," which Paul defined as the "Man of Sin" taking his seat in God's Temple declaring himself to be

God.[169] The Apostle Paul warned the Ephesians to take the whole armor of God so they would be able to withstand "in the Day, the evil one,"[170] referring to the tribulation Jesus warned about.

Revelation describes this time in great detail, using the language of the Mazzaroth. John's vision begins with a view of heaven, with the "Lamb" beside the Father on His throne, unleashing the seven seals. It includes graphic descriptions about the struggle between the multi-headed sea monster and the "woman" (Virgo) who brought forth the man child (Aries), who is to rule the nations with a rod of iron (Leo).

Greek Mythology & Revelation
Cancer in Greek and Roman mythology is known only for its link to Hydra, the multi-headed sea serpent. The constellation Hydra is the longest of all the constellations, stretched out just below the ecliptic the entire length of Virgo and Leo, with its head just beneath Cancer the Crab.

Heracles[171] was sent by Zeus (the supreme god) to defeat Hydra, who was terrorizing the people. In the battle, whenever Heracles would cut off one of Hydra's heads, two more would grow back in its place. Finally, Heracles was able to use a firebrand to cauterize the severed necks as he cut off each of the heads, and finally defeated Hydra. *"While Heracles was fighting the multi-headed monster called the Hydra in the*

---

[169] 2 Thessalonians 2:3-4
[170] Ephesians 6:13
[171] Heracles was a figure of Greek mythology: the Romans took Heracles and changed the name to Hercules, though they did not change the legend.

swamp near Lerna, the crab emerged from the swamp and added its own attack by biting Heracles on the foot. Heracles angrily stamped on the crab, crushing it."[172]

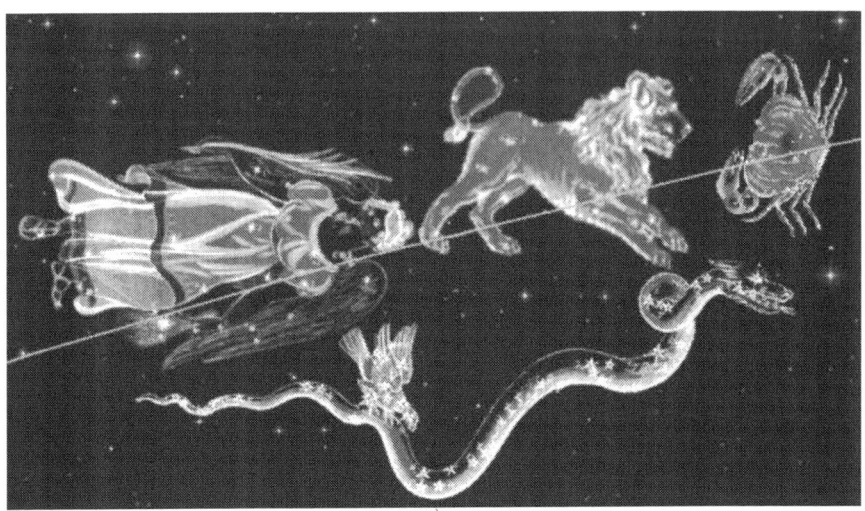

The Greek myth of the struggle between Heracles and Hydra is a corruption of the overthrow of Satan. The giant crab was the agent of Hydra, and represents the Man of Sin (Antichrist) who will persecute the woman (Virgo–representing all of her seed). John tells us that the multi-headed serpent who attempted to attack the woman (described in Revelation 12) gave to the Antichrist (the crab) *"his power, his throne, and great authority."*[173]

In the Greek myth, Hydra does not harm Heracles in any way during the battle. The only harm to Heracles is from the crab attacking his heel. Here is a corruption of the very first

---

[172] Ridpath, Ian, Star Tales, Hydra
[173] Rev 13:2

prophecy in the Bible, spoken to the serpent (Hydra). *"And I will put enmity between you and the woman, And between your seed and her Seed; He shall bruise your head, And you shall bruise His heel."*[174] The "Seed of the woman" (Sarah—Virgo) is the man child, Christ. The "seed" of the serpent is the Antichrist (Cancer). We see this prophecy played out perfectly in the Greek myth of Heracles, Hydra, and Cancer.

The only harm that Satan can do to Jesus Christ is to harm those redeemed by His sacrifice – *"the rest of her [Sarah's] offspring, who keep the commandments of God and have the testimony of Jesus Christ."*[175] The "heel" of Christ is wounded by the Crab's attack on Christ's followers. Many will succumb to this attack of Satan through his surrogate and will fall away, just as Jesus warned. But, others will stand faithful and be preserved through the final fiery trial. Ultimately, the faithful descendants of Sarah will be preserved in the "wilderness" until the very end of the tribulation when Hydra the sea serpent will be defeated by Jesus Christ, as Isaiah graphically describes.

> *Isaiah 26:20-27:1*
> *20 Come, my people, enter your chambers, And shut your doors behind you; Hide yourself, as it were, for a little moment, Until the indignation is past. 21 For behold, the LORD comes out of His place To punish the inhabitants of the earth for their iniquity; The earth will also disclose her blood, And will no more cover her slain.*

---

[174] Gen 3:15
[175] Rev 12:17

27:1 In that day the LORD with His severe sword, great and strong, Will punish Leviathan the fleeing serpent, Leviathan that twisted serpent; And He will slay the reptile that is in the sea.

That Leviathan is the multi-headed Hydra is clear from both the last statement, "the reptile that is in the sea," and from David's seventy-fourth Psalm, "You broke the heads [plural] of Leviathan in pieces."[176]

Isaiah's prophecy was written while the Hydra myth was current among the Greeks. Isaiah lived around 700 BC. The first mention of this myth is from the Greek poet, Hesiod,[177] 800 BC – 700 BC. It is highly likely that Isaiah was well aware of the Greek myth. Isaiah's prophecy was intentionally meant to reference the Greek Hydra myth. Why? Because the One inspiring Isaiah to write was the One who placed Hydra in the constellations in the first place and who had revealed all this long before Isaiah or the Greeks existed. *"By His spirit He hath garnished the heavens; His hand hath formed the crooked serpent."*[178] God and Isaiah knew full well that Hydra represented Satan.

Though the Greeks perverted the original oral prophecy, their myth still contained significant elements of the original truth, despite its corruption and embellishment. By this prophecy — that God would defeat the multi-headed sea serpent after the time of tribulation — Isaiah has given us indisputable proof

---

[176] Psalm 74:14
[177] Hesiod, Theogony, 313
[178] Job 26:13

that the Hydra of Greek mythology and the corresponding constellation were indeed originally meant to represent Satan. And from this bit of evidence we can extrapolate that all of the signs of the zodiac, three of which (Virgo, Leo, Cancer) are linked to Hydra, were originally part of one ancient prophecy given by God to man. Why else would God indicate through Isaiah that He would one day slay a mythological creature? The prophets did not borrow from pagan myths, but rather the pagan myths were corruptions of ancient prophecy, just as Paul charged. *"Because what may be known of God is manifest in them, for God has shown it to them."* And, *"although they knew God, they did not glorify Him as God, nor were thankful, but became futile in their thoughts, and their foolish hearts were darkened. Professing to be wise, they became fools, and changed the glory of the incorruptible God into an image made like corruptible man..."*[179]

There is one more point worth noting about Isaiah's prophecy. He referred to Leviathan (Satan) as both *"Leviathan the fleeing serpent"* and *"Leviathan that twisted serpent."* A serpent is not twisted when fleeing, nor does he "flee" when "twisted." He is twisted (or coiled) when he is attacking his prey, as a python who squeezes the life out of his victims, or a rattlesnake about to strike.

There are three serpents in the constellations. The first is part of Ophiuchus, representing Moses holding the serpent in the wilderness. The other two are Hydra and Draco. Hydra is the "fleeing serpent," stretched out below Virgo, Leo, and Cancer,

---

[179] Romans 1:18-23

parallel to, and just below, the ecliptic. As the earth turns, Hydra "flees" across the sky from east to west. However, Draco revolves around the pole star, never setting. This is Satan's present place of ruler of this earth. *"For you have said in your heart: 'I will ascend into heaven, I will exalt my throne above the stars of God; I will also sit on the mount of the congregation On the farthest sides of the north; I will ascend above the heights of the clouds, I will be like the Most High.' Yet you shall be brought down to Sheol, To the lowest depths of the Pit."*[180]

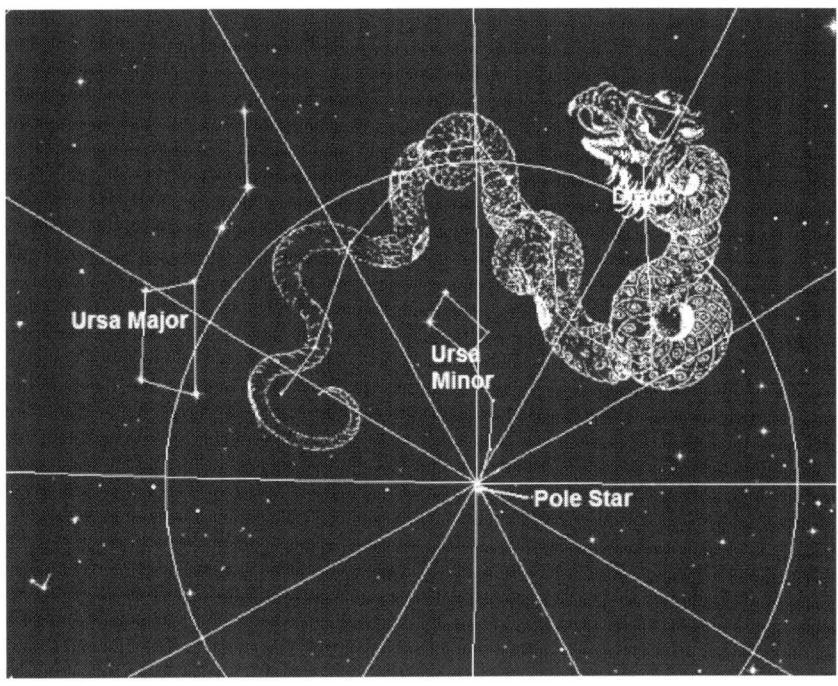

The "twisted (coiled) serpent," represented by Draco, appears to be threatening the constellation known as Ursa Major (the Great Bear), commonly referred to as the "Big Dipper,"

---

[180] Isaiah 14:13-15

chasing it counter-clockwise around the celestial North Pole. The English Bible refers to this constellation as "Arcturus and his sons" (KJV), or the "Great Bear with its cubs" (NKJV).[181] But these are interpretations, not literal translations. In context, God was certainly speaking about constellations. *"Can you bring out Mazzaroth in its season? Or can you guide the Great Bear with its cubs?"* The Hebrew word "aish," rendered "Arcturus" or "Great Bear," literally means "an assembly."[182] The Hebrew text refers to the constellation we call the Big Dipper as "the assembly with its sons." This is what Draco the twisted serpent is poised to strike. In the New Testament, both the words "synagogue" and "Church" mean "an assembly." Draco, who has positioned himself "on the farthest sides of the north," is threatening the assembly of believers. Ursa Minor also appears threatened. It seems the former refers to the Gentile majority and the latter to the Jewish minority within the body of the redeemed.

The Beehive Star Cluster

As noted earlier, perched on the shoulder of Taurus is a star cluster, visible to the naked eye, called the Pleiades. It represents God's provision of the Holy Spirit's power to accompany the apostolic mission to take the Gospel to all nations, confirming the Word with supernatural

---

[181] Job 38:32
[182] Strong's Hebrew Lexicon, #5906 from #5789

signs.[183] There is one other star cluster within the zodiac which is visible to the naked eye. Its modern name is "the Beehive," because it looks like a cluster of bees swarming around their hive, but its ancient Greek name was "Φατνη" (Phatnay). In both Greek and Latin the name of this star cluster means "feeding trough." It is the word rendered "manger" in Luke's Gospel referring to the animal feeding trough used for Jesus' cradle.[184] Kittle says this word was also used in secular Greek to refer to the feeding place of the soldier's campsite — the mess tent.[185]

Why would we have a "feeding trough" pictured in the midst of Cancer? The answer is to be found in John's vision of Hydra's persecution of Virgo in the last days.

> *Rev 12:6, 14-16*
> *6 Then the woman fled into the wilderness, where she has a place prepared by God, that **they should feed her there** one thousand two hundred and sixty days. ...*
> *14 But the woman was given two wings of a great eagle, that she might fly into the wilderness to her place, where she is nourished for a time and times and half a time, from the presence of the serpent.*
> *15 So the serpent spewed water out of his mouth like a flood after the woman, that he might cause her to be carried away by the flood. 16 But the earth helped the woman, and the earth opened its mouth and swallowed up the flood which the dragon had spewed out of his mouth.*

---

[183] Mark 16:20, Hebrews 2:3-4
[184] Luke 2:7
[185] Kittle, Gerhard, Theological Dictionary of the New Testament, Vol. 9, p. 50

Virgo (Sarah) is the mother of the Redeemer (the manchild). She is also the mother of the redeemed, consisting of all who are Abraham's seed through baptism into Jesus Christ.[186] She is given the wings of an eagle to fly into the wilderness to a place of feeding where she will be nourished during the great tribulation. The "feeding trough" star cluster represents the place of safety and nourishment in the wilderness to which she flees. As Isaiah said, *"Come, my people, enter your chambers, And shut your doors behind you; Hide yourself, as it were, for a little moment, Until the indignation is past. For behold, the LORD comes out of His place to punish the inhabitants of the earth for their iniquity."* Immediately after this "little moment" has past, Jesus will *"punish Leviathan the fleeing serpent, Leviathan that twisted serpent; And He will slay the reptile that is in the sea."*

For now, the location of the place "prepared by God" is a secret. It will be revealed at the proper time by the two witnesses who prophesy during the last days.[187] Those who are watching as Jesus commanded will take heed and flee. Just be sure to "remember Lot's wife."[188]

---

[186] Galatians 3:15-18, 26-29

[187] In Revelation 10:3-4, John heard seven thunders proclaim a seven-part prophecy. But he was told not to write down what the seven thunders said. These are things that will be revealed to God's people at the proper time. No doubt, they were withheld because premature knowledge of them would be counterproductive to God's plan (just as God withheld specific knowledge of the crucifixion of Jesus – 1 Cor. 1:2:6-8). Yet, John's acknowledging the messages of the seven thunders tells us that there is further revelation forthcoming. We learn in the very next chapter about God's two prophets who will prophesy for 1,260 days, no doubt providing the missing information.

[188] Luke 17:32

MYSTERY of the MAZZAROTH

Chapter 14
Leo
The King Reigns in Jerusalem

Rev 11:15-18
15 Then the seventh angel sounded: And there were loud voices in heaven, saying, "The kingdoms of this world have become the kingdoms of our Lord and of His Christ, and He shall reign forever and ever!"
16 And the twenty-four elders who sat before God on their thrones fell on their faces and worshiped God, 17 saying: "We give You thanks, O Lord God Almighty, The One who

is and who was and who is to come, Because You have taken Your great power and reigned. 18 The nations were angry, and Your wrath has come, And the time of the dead, that they should be judged, And that You should reward Your servants the prophets and the saints, And those who fear Your name, small and great, And should destroy those who destroy the earth."

Biblical prophecy uses the same pictorial language as the zodiac and identifies its central figure, Jesus Christ, with all three representations of Him in the zodiac. Jesus is the "Branch" in Virgo's right hand, Abraham's promised Seed. The Branch was confirmed in Capricorn as being the descendant of David to reign on David's throne over Abraham's descendants forever. Yet, the "Branch" is clearly linked to both the Lamb (Aries) and the Lion (Leo) by Zechariah and John.

In Pisces, the name of the Branch was revealed through the prophet Zechariah. This was done by Zechariah's fashioning crowns from gold and silver and placing them on the head of the high priest, Joshua. Zechariah then pointed to him declaring: *"Behold! The man, the Branch, the name is in him."* That is, the name of the promised Branch from the kingly line of David was in the high priest, Joshua. The name of the promised Branch seen in Virgo's right hand is therefore *Yeshua* in Hebrew, *Iesous* in Greek, and *Jesus* in English.

In the following passage, there is a similar demonstration, this time performed by an angel with Zechariah observing. Joshua the high priest was seated in the midst of the other priests.

There were twenty-four families of priests that ministered at the Temple,[189] with a patriarch for each of the twenty-four families. Thus, Joshua the High Priest was seated among the twenty-four "elders" of these priestly families. This time a stone was used with seven eyes engraved on it as a sign.

> Zech 3:8-9 NIV
> 8 "'Listen, O high priest Joshua and your associates seated before you, **who are men symbolic of things to come**: I am going to bring my servant, the Branch.
> 9 See, the stone I have set in front of Joshua! **There are seven eyes** on that one stone, and I will engrave an inscription on it,' says the LORD Almighty, 'and I will remove the sin of this land in a single day.

The stone with seven eyes set before Joshua the high priest was a sign, and Joshua and his companion priests were a sign of things to come. Yet, the book of Zechariah does not provide the meaning of this sign. However, John's vision recorded in the book of Revelation does. In doing so, John ties together all three symbols in the zodiac that refer to Jesus Christ – the Branch, the Lamb, and the Lion.

> Rev 5:1-10 NASB
> 1 And I saw in the right hand of Him who sat on the throne a book written inside and on the back, sealed up with seven seals. 2 And I saw a strong angel proclaiming with a loud voice, "Who is worthy to open the book and to break its seals?" 3 And no one in heaven, or on the earth, or under the

---

[189] 1 Chron. 24:1-19

earth, was able to open the book, or to look into it. 4 And I began to weep greatly, because no one was found worthy to open the book, or to look into it; 5 and one of the elders said to me, "Stop weeping; behold, **the Lion that is from the tribe of Judah**, **the Root of David**, has overcome so as to open the book and its seven seals." 6 And I saw between the throne (with the four living creatures) and the elders **a Lamb** standing, as if slain, having seven horns and **seven eyes**, which are the seven Spirits of God, sent out into all the earth. 7 And He came, and He took it out of the right hand of Him who sat on the throne. 8 And when He had taken the book, the four living creatures and the **twenty-four elders** fell down before the Lamb, having each one a harp, and golden bowls full of incense, which are the prayers of the saints. 9 And they sang a new song, saying,

> "Worthy art Thou to take the book, and to break its seals; for Thou wast slain, and didst purchase for God with Thy blood men from every tribe and tongue and people and nation.
> 10 "And Thou hast made them to be a kingdom and priests to our God; and they will reign upon the earth."

The prophet Zechariah saw a vision of a scroll that was very unusual in that it had writing on both sides.[190] Upon the scroll judgments were written. In the above passage, the interpretation of Zechariah's vision was given to John. The scroll that Zechariah had seen was about to be opened by the

---

[190] Zechariah 5:3

only One worthy to execute its judgments. That One was "the Lion of the tribe of Judah." Yet the Lion appeared as a Lamb with seven eyes. According to Zechariah's prophecy, the stone with seven eyes drawn on it was set before Joshua the High Priest, who had been identified as having the name of the "Branch" in him. The book of Revelation gives the final pieces of the riddle in Zechariah. The Branch seen in Virgo that comes from King David's root is named *Yeshua* (Jesus). He has seven eyes, which represent the seven-fold Spirit of God which Isaiah previously prophesied the Messiah would possess.[191] The anointing of the seven-fold Spirit of God was loaned to the Apostles to complete their mission, as represented by the Pleiades perched on Taurus the ox. This Branch named *Jesus* is also the Lamb appearing to John "as though it had been slain." Aries appears in the Dendera zodiac as the sacrificial ram. This Lamb was introduced to John as "the Lion of the tribe of Judah." The song sung by the twenty-four elders and four creatures indicates that He will one day "reign on the earth" along with the redeemed from every nation. In Zechariah, Joshua the high priest seated among his twenty-four companions[192] was a sign representing Jesus reigning on earth among the twenty-four courses of priests at the Temple.[193] Revelation indicates that the redeemed *"shall be priests of God and of Christ, and shall reign with Him a thousand years."*[194]

---

[191] Isaiah 11:1-5
[192] David divided the priests into 24 courses. 1 Chronicles 24:1-19
[193] The 24 elders in heaven are angels who carry out this priestly function on behalf of the saints under Christ, the High Priest "according to the order of Melchisedek." That they are angels is shown by the fact that they are said to offer incense – the prayers of the saints (Rev. 5:8), a priestly function done by angels (Rev. 8:3).
[194] Rev. 20:6

Jesus was called "the Lion of the tribe of Judah" because of Jacob's prophecy. When Jacob was dying, he called his twelve sons and pronounced a prophecy over each one regarding the tribe they would father. When he came to Judah, through whom Jesus' ancestry is traced,[195] he said this: *"Judah, you are he whom your brothers shall praise; Your hand shall be on the neck of your enemies; Your father's children shall bow down before you. Judah is a lion's whelp; From the prey, my son, you have gone up. He bows down, he lies down as a lion; And as a lion, who shall rouse him? The scepter shall not depart from Judah, Nor a lawgiver from between his feet, Until Shiloh comes; And to Him shall be the obedience of the people."*[196] The word "Shiloh" refers to the state of rest and security, the promised everlasting land inheritance God promised Abraham. The new Lawgiver, who holds the scepter of a king, is symbolized by a lion.

Greek Mythology
According to the Greek myth of Heracles and Hydra, all of Hydra's heads were mortal except one, which was immortal. Heracles killed the Hydra, but the one immortal head would not die. So Heracles buried it under a large rock.[197] In the Dendera zodiac, Leo is standing on Hydra, keeping him subdued.

---

[195] Matthew 1:1-17; Luke 3:23-38
[196] Gen 49:8-10
[197] Theoi Greek Mythology, Hydra, http://www.theoi.com/Ther/DrakonHydra.html

MYSTERY of the MAZZAROTH

The book of Revelation indicates that Satan will be defeated and sealed up in the abyss during Christ's Millennial reign. *"Then I saw an angel coming down from heaven, having the key to the bottomless pit and a great chain in his hand. He laid hold of the dragon, that serpent of old, who is the Devil and Satan, and bound him for a thousand years; and he cast him into the bottomless pit, and shut him up, and set a seal on him, so that he should deceive the nations no more till the thousand years were finished. But after these things he must be released for a little while."*[198]

The vulture on Hydra's back depicted in the Dendera Zodiac is also found in the Greek depictions of the constellation, Hydra. At the battle of Armageddon, the vultures will devour the carcasses of Satan's human armies.[199] When his doom is sealed at the battle of Gog after the Millennium, his armies will again be food for the vultures.[200]

---

[198] Revelation 20:1-3
[199] Revelation 19:17-21
[200] Ezekiel 39:1-7 & Revelation 20:7-10

MYSTERY of the MAZZAROTH

The Dendera zodiac depicts a severed leg above Aries' head with a small icon of Aries attached to it. This identifies the severed leg as belonging to Aries – the sacrificial lamb. Similarly, there is a small icon attached to the back of Leo – a king seated on his throne holding the scepter. This indicates that Leo is the promised King.

The Jewish Feasts and the Zodiac

We have seen that the calendar begins on Rosh Hashanah (feast of Trumpets) with the sun in Virgo (which is Jesus' birthday). Also, the sacrifice of the Lamb of God occurred on Passover, when the sun was in the heart of Aries. The sun left Taurus when Jesus ascended to heaven, and entered Gemini when the promised Spirit arrived on the Jewish feast of Pentecost. The fall festivals remain to be fulfilled, including Yom Kippur (the Day of Atonement) and Sukkot (the feast of Tabernacles).

Yom Kippur is the day of Jesus' second coming. We know this because the Apostle Paul indicated that the resurrection of believers will occur when Jesus returns to earth "at the last trumpet."[201]

God commanded the Israelites to keep track of their years in groups of sevens. After farming the land for six years, they were to let the land rest for the seventh year.[202] Like the weekly Sabbath, the yearly Sabbath was based on the creation week, and was also prophetic of six millennia of man's toil under the curse, followed by the seventh millennium, the

---

[201] 1 Corinthians 15:52
[202] Leviticus 23

MYSTERY of the MAZZAROTH

"Sabbath Rest."[203] Each new year was announced on Rosh Hashanah by the blowing of trumpets. The Jewish months were always lunar months, beginning with the new moon. So, Rosh Hashanah always falls on the new moon. But the years were solar years, corrected to the seasons by adding an extra month every few years to keep the year synchronized with the seasons for agricultural purposes. After seven of these 7-year cycles (49 years), God commanded Israel to keep a special year, the 50th year of Jubilee. This rounded out seven Sabbatical cycles from 49 years to an even 50 years.

Yom Kippur (Day of Atonement) was held on the tenth day after Rosh Hashanah, the 10th day of the month Tishri. Its historical significance was to remember the fall of Adam, his banishment from Eden, and the curse upon the earth that resulted. It also looked forward to the day of release from the curse after exactly six thousand years.

Unlike the regular years which began on Rosh Hashanah, the Jubilee year began ten days after the end of the seventh Sabbatical year, on Yom Kippur.

> *Leviticus 25:8-10*
> *8 'And you shall count seven sabbaths of years for yourself, seven times seven years; and the time of the seven sabbaths of years shall be to you forty-nine years.*
> *9 Then **you shall cause the trumpet of the Jubilee to sound on the tenth day of the seventh month; on the***

---

[203] Hebrews 3:7 – 4:11

> *Day of Atonement you shall make the trumpet to sound throughout all your land.*
> *10 And you shall consecrate the fiftieth year, and proclaim liberty throughout all the land to all its inhabitants. It shall be a Jubilee for you; and each of you shall return to his possession, and each of you shall return to his family.*

The last trumpet, which Paul indicated will bring the resurrection of the dead at Jesus' coming, is the Jubilee trumpet. It is the "last trumpet" because the longest cycle kept by the Jews was the Jubilee cycle, and the trumpet was blown at the extreme end of this cycle, ten days after the sounding of the trumpets on Rosh Hashanah. It occurred only once every fifty years. The Jubilee symbolized the removal of the curse from the earth, which Paul describes as the hope for which Christians are to look.[204] The final Jubilee is the beginning of Messiah's Kingdom.

The last of the feasts that God commanded Israel to celebrate is the Feast of Tabernacles. It begins five days after Yom Kippur, and lasts eight days. This feast commemorated Israel's dwelling in tents during their wilderness experience, celebrating that God brought them safely into the Promised Land. It also looks forward to the Millennium, where the promise of the eternal land inheritance will finally be realized.[205] According to Zechariah, this feast will be celebrated in Messiah's Kingdom.

---

[204] Romans 8:14-25
[205] Psalm 37; Hebrews 3-4

MYSTERY of the MAZZAROTH

> *Zech 14:16-21*
> *16 And it shall come to pass that everyone who is left of all the nations which came against Jerusalem shall go up from year to year to worship the King, the LORD of hosts, and to keep the Feast of Tabernacles.*
> *17 And it shall be that whichever of the families of the earth do not come up to Jerusalem to worship the King, the LORD of hosts, on them there will be no rain.*
> *18 If the family of Egypt will not come up and enter in, they shall have no rain; they shall receive the plague with which the LORD strikes the nations who do not come up to keep the Feast of Tabernacles. 19 This shall be the punishment of Egypt and the punishment of all the nations that do not come up to keep the Feast of Tabernacles.*
> *20 In that day "HOLINESS TO THE LORD" shall be engraved on the bells of the horses. The pots in the LORD's house shall be like the bowls before the altar. 21 Yes, every pot in Jerusalem and Judah shall be holiness to the LORD of hosts. Everyone who sacrifices shall come and take them and cook in them. In that day there shall no longer be a Canaanite in the house of the LORD of hosts.*

Interestingly, the festival of Chanukah occurs exactly seventy-five days after Yom Kippur. While God Himself did not command Israel to keep this festival, it was done in response to the miracle of oil God supplied during the time of the Maccabees. When Judah Maccabee cleansed the Temple from the pagan defilement of Antiochus Epiphanies, the menorah burned for eight days on one day's supply of oil until more oil could be manufactured. Ever since then, the Jews have celebrated the eight days of Chanukah, the festival of lights.

The book of Daniel ends with a very curious statement, *"Blessed is he who waits, and comes to the one thousand three hundred and thirty-five days."*[206] The beginning point of this period is the taking away of the daily sacrifice and placing the abomination of desolation by the Antichrist.[207] Revelation indicates a 1,260 day period between this event and the destruction of Antichrist at Jesus' coming.[208] This blessing is pronounced on those who attend a very special event seventy-five days later – the cleansing of the Temple at the beginning of Messiah's rule. It will occur during the eight-day festival of Chanukah, and will be a tremendous blessing for those who attend that Chanukah event.

The Great Jubilee, the Dawning of the Age of Leo

Because the biblical calendar is a luni-solar calendar, the dates of the feasts do not fall on the same days each year according to our Gregorian calendar, which is purely solar (ignoring the lunar cycles). Rosh Hashanah can fall any time between September 5th and October 5th, depending on when the new moon occurs.

As previously explained, precession causes the solstices and equinoxes to creep backwards through the zodiac. At the time of Abraham, the sun was at the feet of Virgo on Rosh Hashanah. This position fluctuates a bit from year to year because Rosh Hashanah is marked by the new moon, and the new moon can appear anytime between September 5th and October 5th. However, over the centuries there has been a

---

[206] Daniel 12:12
[207] cf. Daniel 12:11 & Matthew 24:15
[208] cf. Revelation 12:6, Revelation 13:5, Revelation 19:20-21

continuous progression up Virgo's body. By the time of Jesus' birth two thousand years later, the sun was roughly mid-body in Virgo (her womb). Now, two millennia after Jesus, the sun is leaving Virgo and entering Leo on Rosh Hashanah. Because Rosh Hashanah is calculated by the new moon which fluctuates relative to the solar position, currently Rosh Hashanah sometimes occurs with the sun in Virgo and sometimes in Leo. If the new moon appears between September 5th and 15th, the sun is in Leo on Rosh Hashanah. If it occurs between September 16th and October 5th, the sun is in Virgo on Rosh Hashanah.

Yom Kippur, the Day of Jesus' second coming when the last Jubilee trumpet will sound, occurs ten days after Rosh Hashanah. The sun is almost always in Virgo on Yom Kippur. However, precession has caused the sun to now be bordering on Leo on Yom Kippur every several years, when Rosh Hashanah falls on the earliest possible day of the year (September 5th or 6th). The sun is just barely beginning to enter Leo on Yom Kippur and before long it will do so more frequently. We are on the verge of entering the age of Leo, when Christ will reign on the Throne of David!

Astrologers claim that we are now in the age of Pisces, about to enter the age of Aquarius, but they are making three major mistakes. First, they use a solar calendar rather than the Jewish luni-solar calendar. Consequently, they ignore the new moon. Second, they use an artificially-divided zodiac, where each zodiac sign covers thirty degrees exactly, rather than considering that some zodiac constellations are much larger than others. Dividing the twelve signs of the zodiac into twelve equal segments of 30 degrees each is an invention of Greek astrology. It is not what we actually observe in the heavens. Third, the precession marker they are following through the zodiac is the spring equinox, but this is not the biblical marker. The correct marker is the sun's location in the zodiac on a specific date – the date of the fall of man and the date of Jesus' second coming (Yom Kippur).

It has taken about four thousand years (since Abraham) for precession to move the sun through Virgo on Rosh Hashanah. Interestingly, during each year it takes the sun fifty days to move through Virgo, the same number of days as there are years in a Jubilee cycle.

The age of Virgo began shortly after the flood, about four thousand years ago, when God first appeared to Abraham and made His promises to him and to his Seed. Its mid-point was the birth of Jesus Christ, when the sun was in Virgo's womb on Rosh Hashanah — Jesus' birthday – and it will end with the dawning of the age of Leo.

The Dendera Zodiac & the Age of Leo

We saw in the introduction that the alignment of the zodiacal signs with the solstices and equinoxes in the Dendera zodiac indicate a date of about 2,300 BC, the time of the great flood according to the Hebrew Bible.

The Dendera zodiac also points to a future date, the dawn of the age of Leo. It does this by repeating the sign of Leo just outside the circle of the zodiacal signs. The secondary image of Leo is not standing, as is the primary zodiacal Leo. He is seated, with his front paws on the Egyptian symbol for water. One of the major features of Messiah's Kingdom is that a river of healing water will flow from Messiah's Throne, along which banks will grow the Tree of Life. [209] This water will flow down into the Dead Sea, which will then be "healed" and become an abundant source of fish for food.

---

[209] Ezekiel 47:1-12; Rev. 22:1-3

MYSTERY of the MAZZAROTH

The secondary image of Leo appears with its edge just coming into alignment with the fall equinox. Precession has brought Leo into this position in our time, the first half of the twenty-first century, as the circle of zodiac signs in the Dendera zodiac has rotated clockwise. As stated before, the position of Leo (and all of the zodiac signs), in relation to the equinoxes and solstices, depicts a date of about 2300 BC, which was the time of Noah's flood. The secondary position of Leo, seated with His front paws on the symbol for water, depicts the first half of the 21st century by its alignment with the fall equinox. Thus, the space between the primary and secondary Leo is the time between the first judgment of the world by flood and the second judgment of the world by fire (when Messiah's Kingdom arrives).

Josephus indicated that the sons of Seth built monuments to preserve their knowledge of astronomy in light of the two coming universal judgments, one by flood and one by fire. Peter warned that just as the first judgment of the flood overtook the scoffers by surprise, so also would the judgment by fire on the Day of the Lord.[210] What a coincidence that the only two discernible dates in the Dendera zodiac, based on the alignment of the zodiac constellations with the equinoxes and solstices, depict the time of the great flood and the coming Day of the Lord. The Dendera zodiac may very well have copied and preserved some of the most ancient astronomy of the sons of Seth, passed on through Noah and his descendants to Abraham, and from Abraham to the Egyptians.

---

[210] 2 Peter 3:1-12

Chapter 15
Epilogue

In deciding a civil case, the jury is instructed by the judge to evaluate the evidence and come to a verdict based on the preponderance of the evidence. In many cases, there is no smoking gun or absolute proof. Circumstantial evidence is sufficient to reach a verdict if it reaches a certain threshold.

In this study of the zodiac, many inferences have been drawn from circumstantial evidence. Some might argue that the connections made between biblical prophecy, the zodiacal signs, mythology, and the Dendera artifact are all just coincidences. Yet these connections are too obvious and too numerous to ignore. Some of the clearest and most remarkable biblical references to prophecy in the zodiac are the attack on Virgo by the multi-headed serpent mentioned in Revelation 12, and Hydra's defeat at the second coming described in Isaiah 27.

The opponents of Christianity are not shy about making similar connections between pagan mythology and the story of the Bible in order to support their claim that the Bible is not original, but has borrowed many components from paganism. It seems that such similarities are convincing to the anti-Christian so long as he is able to use these connections to attack Christianity. Therefore, use of similar comparisons to defend Christianity cannot be criticized on the grounds that insufficient circumstantial evidence has been shown. Indeed, there are too many similarities between pagan myths and the story of the Bible to be mere coincidence.

The question to be decided is not whether ideas have been borrowed or that connections exist. We have seen many such connections. The question to be settled is, "What do these connections mean?"

Opponents of Christianity sometimes claim this evidence proves that Christianity is not original, but is a corruption and evolution of paganism. Yet, the truth is just the reverse. Paganism is a knockoff and corruption of Christianity. The key to proving this is demonstrating that the relevant components of Christianity were revealed first, before the pagan myths originated. Opponents of Christianity have conveniently forgotten the most important component of Christianity — predictive prophecy and its antiquity. God has revealed His plan for mankind in general, and Israel in particular, through the prophets. The oldest recorded prophecy is from Enoch (as quoted by Jude), who lived before the flood – before the Sumerian, Babylonian, Egyptian, or Greek cultures arose. Moses recorded many prophecies also, well before Greek mythologies arose.

The early Christians were confronted with the very same charge, that the new religion spreading throughout the Roman Empire was similar to some of the Greek myths. Justin Martyr, writing only a few decades after John's death, made an unassailable defense of Christianity, demonstrating that the Greek poets had plagiarized the Hebrew prophets who prophesied of the coming of Christ.

"There were, then, among the Jews certain men who were prophets of God, through whom the prophetic Spirit published beforehand things that were to come to pass, ere ever they happened. And their prophecies, as they were spoken and when they were uttered, the kings who happened to be reigning among the Jews at the several times carefully preserved in their possession, when they had been arranged in books by the prophets themselves in their own Hebrew language.

And when Ptolemy king of Egypt formed a library, and endeavored to collect the writings of all men, he heard also of these prophets, and sent to Herod, who was at that time king of the Jews, requesting that the books of the prophets be sent to him. And Herod the king did indeed send them, written, as they were, in the foresaid Hebrew language. And when their contents were found to be unintelligible to the Egyptians, he again sent and requested that men be commissioned to translate them into the Greek language. And when this was done, the books remained with the Egyptians, where they are until now. They are also in the possession of all Jews throughout the world; ...

In these books, then, of the prophets we found Jesus our Christ foretold as coming, born of a virgin, growing up to man's estate, and healing every disease and every sickness, and raising the dead, and being hated, and unrecognized, and crucified, and dying, and rising again, and ascending into heaven, and being, and being called, the Son of God. We find it also predicted that certain persons should be sent by Him into every nation to publish these things, and that

> *rather among the Gentiles [than among the Jews] men should believe on Him. And He was predicted before He appeared, first 5000 years before,[211] and again 3000, then 2000, then 1000, and yet again 800; for in the succession of generations prophets after prophets arose."*[212]

Justin went on in the following chapters to point out many specific prophecies about Jesus Christ, all of which had been recorded before the Greek myths, concluding with this:

> *"Though we could bring forward many other prophecies, we forbear, judging these sufficient for the persuasion of those who have ears to hear and understand; and considering also that those persons are able to see that we do not make mere assertions without being able to produce proof, like those fables that are told of the so-called sons of Jupiter. For with what reason should we believe of a crucified man that He is the first-born of the unbegotten God, and Himself will pass judgment on the whole human race, unless we had found testimonies concerning Him published before He came and was born as man, and unless we saw that things had happened accordingly — the devastation of the land of the Jews, and men of every race persuaded by His teaching through the apostles..."*[213]

---

[211] The dates given by Justin are calculated from the ages of the patriarchs given in the Septuagint (Greek Old Testament). These are much longer than those in the Hebrew originals. While this might affect the date of Enoch (which Justin puts at 5,000 BC), it does not affect the date of Abraham, Moses, or the prophets who preceded the earliest Greek poets.
[212] Justin Martyr, First Apology, XXXI
[213] Justin Martyr, First Apology, LIII

Justin pointed to the stark contrast between Christianity and the Greek mythologies. Christianity provided documentation by means of recorded and verifiable prophecies. The pagan myths provided no documentation whatsoever, not even that the events they describe actually occurred, never mind giving prophecies that actually came to pass.

> *"But those who hand down the myths which the poets have made, adduce no proof to the youths who learn them; and we proceed to demonstrate that they have been uttered by the influence of the wicked demons, to deceive and lead astray the human race. For having heard it proclaimed through the prophets that the Christ was to come, and that the ungodly among men were to be punished by fire, they put forward many to be called sons of Jupiter, under the impression that they would be able to produce in men the idea that the things which were said with regard to Christ were mere marvelous tales, like the things which were said by the poets. And these things were said both among the Greeks and among all nations where they [the demons] heard the prophets foretelling that Christ would specially be believed in; but that in hearing what was said by the prophets they did not accurately understand it, but imitated what was said of our Christ, like men who are in error, we will make plain.*
>
> *The prophet Moses, then, was, as we have already said, older than all [pagan] writers; and by him, as we have also said before, it was thus predicted: "There shall not fail a prince from Judah, nor a lawgiver from between his feet, until He come for whom it is reserved; and He shall be the desire of the Gentiles, binding His foal to the vine, washing His robe in*

the blood of the grape." The devils, accordingly, when they heard these prophetic words, said that Bacchus was the son of Jupiter, and gave out that he was the discoverer of the vine, and they number wine [or, the ass] among his mysteries; and they taught that, having been torn in pieces, he ascended into heaven. And because in the prophecy of Moses it had not been expressly intimated whether He who was to come was the Son of God, and whether He would, riding on the foal, remain on earth or ascend into heaven, and because the name of "foal" could mean either the foal of an ass or the foal of a horse, they, not knowing whether He who was foretold would bring the foal of an ass or of a horse as the sign of His coming, nor whether He was the Son of God, as we said above, or of man, gave out that Bellerophon, a man born of man, himself ascended to heaven on his horse Pegasus. And when they heard it said by the other prophet Isaiah, that He should be born of a virgin, and by His own means ascend into heaven, they pretended that Perseus was spoken of. And when they knew what was said, as has been cited above, in the prophecies written aforetime, "Strong as a giant to run his course," they said that Hercules was strong, and had journeyed over the whole earth. And when, again, they learned that it had been foretold that He should heal every sickness, and raise the dead, they produced Aesculapius.[214]

In following chapters, Justin went on to show that even the Greek philosopher Plato borrowed many of his ideas from Moses.

---

[214] Justin Martyr, First Apology, LIV

MYSTERY of the MAZZAROTH

In his Hortatory Address to the Greeks, Justin again contrasted Christianity and the Greek myths, this time documenting his claims from ancient Greek sources that were extant in his day, and available to his readers. He proved the familiarity of the ancient Greek poets with the Hebrews and their first prophet, Moses.

> *"I will begin, then, with our first prophet and lawgiver, Moses; first explaining the times in which he lived, on authorities which among you are worthy of all credit. For I do not propose to prove these things only from our own divine histories, which as yet you are unwilling to credit on account of the inveterate error of your forefathers, but also from your own histories, and such, too, as have no reference to our worship, that you may know that, of all your teachers, whether sages, poets, historians, philosophers, or lawgivers, by far the oldest, as the Greek histories show us, was Moses, who was our first religious teacher.*
>
> *For in the times of Ogyges and Inachus, whom some of your poets suppose to have been earth-born, Moses is mentioned as the leader and ruler of the Jewish nation. For in this way he is mentioned both by Polemon in the first book of his Hellenics, and by Apion son of Posidonius in his book against the Jews, and in the fourth book of his history, where he says that during the reign of Inachus over Argos the Jews revolted from Amasis king of the Egyptians, and that Moses led them. And Ptolemaeus the Mendesian, in relating the history of Egypt, concurs in all this.*

And those who write the Athenian history, Hellanicus and Philochorus (the author of The Attic History), Castor and Thallus and Alexander Polyhistor, and also the very well informed writers on Jewish affairs, Philo and Josephus, have mentioned Moses as a very ancient and time-honored prince of the Jews. Josephus, certainly, desiring to signify even by the title of his work the antiquity and age of the history, wrote thus at the commencement of the history: "The Jewish antiquities of Flavius Josephus," — signifying the oldness of the history by the word "antiquities."

And your most renowned historian Diodorus, who employed thirty whole years in epitomizing the libraries, and who, as he himself wrote, traveled over both Asia and Europe for the sake of great accuracy, and thus became an eye-witness of very many things, wrote forty entire books of his own history. And he in the first book, having said that he had learned from the Egyptian priests that Moses was an ancient lawgiver, and even the first, wrote of him in these very words: "For subsequent to the ancient manner" of living in Egypt which gods and heroes are fabled to have regulated, they say that Moses first persuaded the people to use written laws, and to live by them; and he is recorded to have been a man both great of soul and of great faculty in social matters." Then, having proceeded a little further, and wishing to mention the ancient lawgivers, he mentions Moses first. For he spoke in these words: "Among the Jews they say that Moses ascribed his laws to that God who is called Jehovah, whether because they judged it a marvelous and quite divine conception which promised to benefit a multitude of men, or because they were of opinion that the people would be the more obedient when they contemplated the majesty and power of those who were said to have invented the laws.

And they say that Sasunchis was the second Egyptian legislator, a man of excellent understanding. And the third, they say, was Sesonchosis the king, who not only performed the most brilliant military exploits of any in Egypt, but also consolidated that warlike race by legislation. And the fourth lawgiver, they say, was Bocchoris the king, a wise and surpassingly skillful man. And after him it is said that Amasis the king acceded to the government, whom they relate to have regulated all that pertains to the rulers of provinces, and to the general administration of the government of Egypt. And they say that Darius, the father of Xerxes, was the sixth who legislated for the Egyptians."[215]

Justin's argument is unassailable. He cited extant ancient sources, both Greek and Egyptian, to prove the antiquity of Moses. He cited the Septuagint, the Greek translation of the books of Moses and the Prophets made three centuries before Christ appeared, where these prophecies could be read in Greek. Justin's readers were able to access these historical documents, none of which had been produced by Christians. They were part of the historical record. They confirmed the antiquity of Moses and the Prophets, as well as a Greek translation of their prophecies concerning the Christ who was to come.

---

[215] Justin Martyr, Hortatory Address to the Greeks, IX

Someone might point out that the Babylonians also had myths, some of which may have predated Moses. Yet it is clear that these myths sprang from the original signs of the zodiac. As has been demonstrated throughout this book, the zodiac tells the same story as the Hebrew prophets, in the same order, using the same symbols. The zodiac signs themselves were merely mnemonic devices used in telling the original prophetic story orally. There was already a body of oral tradition, accompanied by the zodiac signs, which antedates all religions from all regions of the earth, and this story is consistent with the Bible. Therefore, it is no leap of logic to claim that major details about the coming Messiah known through the Hebrew prophets were also known through this prior oral tradition. There is nothing in any of the ancient myths or mystery religions that predates God's revelation of His plan of redemption, of which Christianity is the fulfillment.

A Challenge to Agnostics
For some people, nothing short of absolute proof will suffice. Even then, what constitutes "absolute proof" will certainly be disputed. Others are easily persuaded, sometimes easily fooled, by a reasonably good presentation of subjectively selected "facts." Neither group is likely to be successful in the pursuit of truth.

The agnostic needs to face his own bias and whether he is really interested in truth. Most people are only superficially interested in truth, as long as it does not demand too much of them. If the burden of knowing the truth is too great, they opt for a convenient lie or willful ignorance.

MYSTERY of the MAZZAROTH

The Apostle Paul in the first chapter of Romans made a remarkably bold claim. He wrote that the overall cause of the degrading of God's original revelation to man could be traced to one very specific thing: People did not like to retain God in their thinking because of the responsibility to God which that brings to human actions. *"For since the creation of the world His invisible attributes are clearly seen, being understood by the things that are made, even His eternal power and Godhead, so that they are without excuse, because, although they knew God, **they did not glorify Him as God**, nor were thankful, but became futile in their thoughts, and their foolish hearts were darkened."*[216] Paul put the blame for their muddied and confused thinking squarely on them. They did not want truth. Instead, they *"exchanged the truth of God for the lie,"* and *"they did not like to retain God in their knowledge,"* so *"God gave them over to a debased mind."* A significant part of the problem was their rejection of the gender roles that God had ordained at creation.

If Paul was right, then one's personal bias in this area stands in the way of clear thinking and objectivity, and is a major impediment to the pursuit of truth. If one fails to find the truth regarding God's existence and whether He will indeed judge all men, he risks the wrath and condemnation of God.

The question that ought to be asked by someone questioning God's existence is this: What kind of evidence would the God portrayed in the Bible give? He is presented in Scripture as God who desires a personal relationship with those whom He created in His own image. Logically, we should expect the

---

[216] Rom. 1:20-21

evidence He provided to be the kind of evidence that engenders us to trust Him in a personal relationship. Trust is based on a consistent record – faithfulness in keeping one's word.

Looking at Scripture, there is a long record of God's interaction with a select group of people — the nation that sprang from the loins of Abraham through Sarah. That nation still exists today. It is not difficult to judge whether God's claims about that nation are true, whether Israel's history bears out God's making good on His promises and threats, and whether Israel's modern history is consistent with what God has said. This historical record is spread over four-thousand years. It gives a very good body of evidence to assess this God and decide whether He deserves our trust or whether He is the figment of a collective consciousness. Israel has survived all these centuries against incredible odds, just as God promised.[217] Yet, she has suffered in exile also, just as He threatened. She has never had, and will never have, peace and permanent possession of the land until she acknowledges her Messiah, Jesus. Forty years before the Romans destroyed Jerusalem and the Temple, Jesus warned, *"If you had known, even you, especially in this your day, the things that make for your peace! But now they are hidden from your eyes. For days will come upon you when your enemies will build an embankment around you, surround you and close you in on every side, and level you, and your children within you, to the ground; and they will not leave in you one stone upon another, because you did not know the time of your visitation."*[218] Jesus' prophecy was fulfilled to the letter,

---

[217] Genesis 17:7; Psalm 89:34-37; Isaiah 49:14-16
[218] Luke 19:42-44

when Titus and the Roman armies leveled Jerusalem and the Temple. He predicted that *"Jerusalem will be trodden down by the nations until the times of the nations are fulfilled."*[219] That has indeed been the state of Jerusalem ever since.

The zodiac is a part of history also. It has spoken the same language and message as the Hebrew prophets, providing a parallel historical record. This pictorial record was also given in advance of the events it depicts, providing a basis for trusting its designer. If the Designer was faithful in bringing the various signs of the zodiac to fruition throughout Israel's history, there is every reason to assume He will complete the last two signs. Are you ready for that eventuality?

Both Scripture and the zodiac approach revelation on the same human level, building trust in the One behind them by methodical faithfulness. If the God of the Bible is real, He has acted consistently with His stated objective and with His revealed attributes for several thousand years. No human being can fabricate this history or its record; it is preserved in a multitude of ancient manuscripts, engraved in stone, and been uncovered in a plethora of archeological sites.

The God of the Bible has been consistent over several millennia. What He said to Abraham is consistent with what He said through Jesus Christ two-thousand years later. Isaiah's prophecies agree with John's prophecies written eight hundred years later. Each of the prophets, spread out over many centuries, provides pieces of a grand puzzle that

---

[219] Luke 21:24

requires all of them. None of them could have known the entire big picture until the very last one. Yet, they all agree, each adding critical pieces to the whole.

Paul was right after all. *"For since the creation of the world His invisible attributes are clearly seen, being understood by the things that are made, even His eternal power and Godhead, so that they are without excuse, because, although they knew God, they did not glorify Him as God, nor were thankful, but became futile in their thoughts, and their foolish hearts were darkened. Professing to be wise, they became fools, and changed the glory of the incorruptible God into an image made like corruptible man — and birds and four-footed animals and creeping things. Therefore God also gave them up to uncleanness, in the lusts of their hearts, to dishonor their bodies among themselves, who exchanged the truth of God for the lie, and worshiped and served the creature rather than the Creator, who is blessed forever. Amen.*

While ignorance may indeed be bliss, the reader can no longer claim ignorance. Substantial evidence for the existence of God has been provided. The supernatural nature of accurate predictive prophecy, both spread across the heavens and written in the Hebrew prophets, provides absolute proof. Agnosticism is not an option.

A Challenge to Jews who Reject Jesus Christ
The New Testament is the fulfillment of what the Hebrew prophets foresaw. Many parallels have been drawn between the prophets and the signs of the zodiac. These provide a solid basis for concluding that Israel's history was indeed foretold in advance across the heavens. The zodiac portrays the

Abrahamic Covenant, the giving of the Law of Moses, the wilderness wandering, the conquering of the land by Joshua, the Davidic Covenant, the Babylonian captivity, and the return from captivity. Yet, the Mazzaroth does not stop with Pisces, skipping over Aries, Taurus, Gemini, and Cancer in getting to Leo. All of these deal with the work of Jesus Christ, the Messiah of Israel.

The Hebrew prophet, Zechariah, named the Messiah, Yeshua (Jesus), five hundred years before He was born. Is this any less impressive than God's naming Cyrus the Great two hundred years before he was born? The Hebrew prophet, Isaiah, described the Lamb (Aries) as the sacrifice for the sins of Isaiah's people. This sacrificial Lamb becomes the One who inherits all things.[220] Isaiah predicted that the Jews and their rabbis would reject his report,[221] that they would despise the Lamb of God, and consider His death to be justified by the Law of Moses.[222] Indeed, Isaiah's words have come to pass.

Moses predicted the coming of another prophet and Lawgiver.[223] Isaiah confirmed that the Gentiles would receive His Law.

> *"Behold! My Servant whom I uphold, My Elect One in whom My soul delights! I have put My Spirit upon Him; He will bring forth justice to the Gentiles. He will not cry out, nor raise His voice, Nor cause His voice to be heard in the*

---

[220] Isaiah 53:12
[221] Isaiah 53:1
[222] Isaiah 53:2-4
[223] Deuteronomy 18:15-19

street. *A bruised reed He will not break, And smoking flax He will not quench; He will bring forth justice for truth. He will not fail nor be discouraged, Till He has established justice in the earth; And the coastlands shall wait for His law. Thus says God the LORD, Who created the heavens and stretched them out, Who spread forth the earth and that which comes from it, Who gives breath to the people on it, And spirit to those who walk on it: "I, the LORD, have called You in righteousness, And will hold Your hand; I will keep You and give You as a covenant to the people, As a light to the Gentiles, To open blind eyes, To bring out prisoners from the prison, Those who sit in darkness from the prison house. I am the LORD, that is My name; And My glory I will not give to another, Nor My praise to carved images. Behold, the former things have come to pass, And new things I declare; Before they spring forth I tell you of them."* [224]

The Gentiles have received Jesus as the Messiah, the new Lawgiver.

Micah predicted that the Messiah would be born in Bethlehem, the city of David. Is it a coincidence that Jesus was born there? *"But you, Bethlehem Ephrathah, Though you are little among the thousands of Judah, Yet out of you shall come forth to Me The One to be Ruler in Israel, Whose goings forth are from of old, From everlasting."* [225]

---

[224] Isaiah 42:5-9
[225] Micah 5:2

Does not the twenty-second Psalm predict in exact detail the crucifixion of Jesus?[226] The sixteenth verse says, *"They pierced My hands and My feet."* Yet, Jewish translations read, *"like a lion they are at my hands and feet."*[227] The Christian Bible's reading comes from the Septuagint. Which is correct? The Dead Sea Scrolls prove that the Christian Bible is correct and the Jewish Bible is in error here. *"Psalm 22 is a favorite among Christians since it is often linked to the New Testament with the suffering and death of Jesus. A well-known and controversial reading is found in verse 16, where the Masoretic Text reads, 'Like a lion are my hands and feet,' whereas the Septuagint has, "They have pierced my hands and feet.' Among the scrolls the reading in question is found only in Nahal Hever (abbreviated 5/6HevPs), which reads, 'They have pierced my hands and my feet'!"*[228]

The words of the Hebrew prophets and the sequence of signs in the zodiac require all Jews to take a second look at the claims of Jesus Christ and the New Testament. There is no other atonement for sin than the Lamb of God.

A Challenge to Christians

Much wrong and damaging theology has been foisted upon Christianity over the last two millennia. Some of it sprang from Greek philosophy and Gnosticism. The Jewishness of Jesus, the Apostles, and the whole New Testament has been largely purged from Christianity and replaced with Greek mysticism. The simple hope of Abraham — that both he and

---

[226] Compare Psalm 22 to Matthew 27:32-56
[227] Psalm 22:17, The Holy Scriptures, Jewish Publication Society of America, 1917
[228] Martin Abegg, Jr., Peter Flint & Eugene Ulrich, The Dead Sea Scrolls Bible, pp. 518-519

his Seed would inherit the land from the Nile to the Euphrates as an everlasting possession[229] — has been discarded by Christianity. It has been replaced with the Platonic-Gnostic idea of escaping the material creation and ascending into the heavens. The Bible teaches that Creation itself is the inheritance of Jesus Christ and all who are joined to Him.[230] It is to be restored and the curse lifted. This restored earth will be the permanent home of both God and man.[231] Those baptized into Jesus Christ have become "Abraham's seed, and heirs according to the promise,"[232] fulfilling the portion of the Abrahamic promise that all nations would be blessed through Abraham's Seed, Jesus Christ. The promise is not heaven, but the restored land as an everlasting possession.[233]

One of the reasons the zodiac has been misinterpreted by Rolleston, Seiss, Bullinger, Kennedy, Missler, et al, is because their theology either ignores Israel's central role entirely in God's plan to restore His creation, or ignores the union of Jew and Gentile in the Abrahamic promises.

The last two signs of the zodiac, Cancer and Leo, foretell two very inconvenient chapters in God's prophetic program. Dispensationalists do not know how to deal with the time of tribulation for Jesus' elect foretold in Cancer and God's preservation of His own during that time. Amillennialists do

---

[229] Genesis 15:18; Deuteronomy 1:7-8; Deuteronomy 11:24
[230] Acts 3:19-21; Romans 8:16-25; Galatians 3:16-29; Hebrews 3:7 – 4:11
[231] cf. Exodus 25:8; Exodus 29:46; Ezekiel 37:25-28; Ezekiel 43:7; Revelation 7:15; Revelation 21:3
[232] Galatians 3:28-29
[233] cf. Genesis 13:15, Genesis 17:8 & Paul's quotation from the LXX and interpretation in Galatians 3:16

not know how to deal with the renovation of the earth and fulfillment of the promise to Abraham of the permanent possession of the Land foretold in Leo.

It's time to awake out of sleep. The end times are upon us. There is a brief trial to be endured, followed by the realization of the blessing that God promised to Abraham and all who are "Abraham's seed," both Jew and Gentile.

> *Isaiah 40:10-11, 21-31*
> *10 Behold, the Lord GOD shall come with a strong hand, And His arm shall rule for Him; Behold, His reward is with Him, And His work before Him.*
> *11 He will feed His flock like a shepherd; He will gather the lambs with His arm, And carry them in His bosom, And gently lead those who are with young. ...*
> *21 Have you not known? Have you not heard? Has it not been told you from the beginning? Have you not understood from the foundations of the earth?*
> *22 It is He who sits above the circle of the earth, And its inhabitants are like grasshoppers, Who stretches out the heavens like a curtain, And spreads them out like a tent to dwell in.*
> *23 He brings the princes to nothing; He makes the judges of the earth useless.*
> *24 Scarcely shall they be planted, Scarcely shall they be sown, Scarcely shall their stock take root in the earth, When He will also blow on them, And they will wither, And the whirlwind will take them away like stubble.*
> *25 "To whom then will you liken Me, Or to whom shall I be equal?" says the Holy One.*

26 Lift up your eyes on high, And see who has created these things, Who brings out their host by number; He calls them all by name, By the greatness of His might And the strength of His power; Not one is missing.

27 Why do you say, O Jacob, And speak, O Israel: "My way is hidden from the LORD, And my just claim is passed over by my God"?

28 Have you not known? Have you not heard? The everlasting God, the LORD, The Creator of the ends of the earth, Neither faints nor is weary. His understanding is unsearchable.

29 He gives power to the weak, And to those who have no might He increases strength.

30 Even the youths shall faint and be weary, And the young men shall utterly fall,

31 But those who wait on the LORD Shall renew their strength; They shall mount up with wings like eagles, They shall run and not be weary, They shall walk and not faint.

Solo Christo

MYSTERY of the MAZZAROTH

The time of the coming of Messiah to establish His Kingdom on Earth has been the "Holy Grail" of Bible prophecy since Daniel first inquired. He was told that this knowledge was sealed up "until the TIME of the END," but when revealed, "the wise will understand."

The earliest Christians claimed a tradition from the Apostles that the Kingdom of Messiah would come exactly 6000 years from creation. The New Testament books of Hebrews and 2 Peter confirm this claim, showing it was taught by the Apostles just prior to the destruction of Jerusalem. If we can determine what year we are in on a continuous calendar counting from creation, we can know the year of Jesus' return.

Virtually all previous biblical chronologies have used a mixture of biblical and secular histories. The reliance on secular histories was because of a mistaken belief that the Bible does not contain chronological data for the period from Cyrus the Great to Artaxerxes, or from the crucifixion to the second coming. Yet, there is no missing data. The Bible contains everything necessary for a complete chronology from creation to the second coming.

Jesus instructed pastors and elders to "become ready" by discovering the time of His coming so they can feed His flock "the necessary food at the proper time." He gave a dire warning to those who refuse to do so. However, for those who heed Jesus' warning, He promised to make them ruler over all that He has in His Kingdom.

Made in the USA
Lexington, KY
14 November 2013